Did The Catholic Church

Give Us The Bible?

THE TRUE HISTORY OF GOD'S WORDS

DAVID W. DANIELS

ILLUSTRATIONS BY JACK CHICK

CHICK
PUBLICATIONS
Ontario, Calif. 91761

For a complete list of distributors near you,
call us at (909) 987-0771, or visit us online at:
www.chick.com

Copyright © 2005 David W. Daniels

Published by:
CHICK PUBLICATIONS
P. O. Box 3500, Ontario, Calif. 91761-1019 USA
Tel: (909) 987-0771
Fax: (909) 941-8128
Web: www.chick.com
Email: postmaster@chick.com

Printed in the United States of America

First Printing

ISBN: 0-7589-0579-3

Table of Contents

APPENDIX
Extra Reading and References

INDEXES

DID SHE REALLY?

Did the Roman Catholic church <u>really</u> give us the Bible?

Or did God give us the Bible in some other way?

"Saint" Augustine

Erasmus

Let's find out!

**History shows there are TWO Bibles
with two histories—not just one.
And these Bibles <u>do</u> <u>not</u> <u>agree</u> with each other.
How do we know *which one* is from God?**

I need **Mother Church** and her **scholars** to tell me **which** Bible is correct and what it **means**.

Augustine of Hippo
(354-430AD)

No, **God** showed us which to believe by **preserving His words** through His faithful followers.

<u>NO</u> church is above the Bible!

Desiderius Erasmus
(1466-1536AD)

It comes down to this:
Either you trust **God** and what He *said*,
or you trust **man's** opinion about what God *meant*.
This is a choice you MUST make.

BELIEVERS ARE TOTALLY IN THE DARK OVER THIS ISSUE, BECAUSE THE TRUTH HAS BEEN CLOUDED OVER.

Like it or not ... we are surrounded by false teachers
(God calls them "ravening wolves" [1])
who are slowly destroying our faith.

Did God *really* saaaaay that?

**Unless you know about history
as it <u>actually</u> happened, *you also* will fall
under the spell of these deceivers.**

[1] See Matthew 7:14

Chapter One:

A Short History of the Bible— God's Own Words

A QUICK SUMMARY

God wrote the Ten Commandments—*twice*—
with His own finger![1]

What about all the **other** books of the Bible?

"All Scripture is given by inspiration of God ..."[2]

—Either way, **GOD** wrote the Bible.

---

[1] See Exodus 31:18;32:15-16; 34:1-5.
[2] See 2 Timothy 3:16-17. Also see Appendix A, "For Further Reading."

The ***first*** time a person writes something, it's called an "**original autograph.**" <u>ANYTHING ELSE IS A "COPY."</u>

When God revealed His laws to Moses, He wrote the <u>first</u> <u>ten</u> on two tables of stone—on <u>both</u> <u>sides</u>.[1]

1.

2.

Front   Back

Moses brought them down from Mount Sinai in Arabia,[2] to show all the Israelites what God had written.

But when he came down, he found the people were worshiping a <u>golden</u> <u>calf</u>—not God—also drinking and dancing before it. Moses was <u>so</u> <u>angry</u> that "<u>he</u> <u>cast</u> <u>the</u> <u>tables</u> out of his hands, <u>and</u> <u>brake</u> <u>them</u> beneath the mount."[3]

Boy, did Moses have a <u>headache</u>! But God told him,
**"TAKE TWO TABLETS,
AND CALL ON ME IN THE MORNING."[4]**

And so he did. Now Moses had to cut <u>his</u> <u>own</u> tables. Then God **copied** the <u>same</u> <u>words</u>[5] on the <u>second</u> set.

---

[1] See Exodus 32:15.
[2] See Galatians 4:25.
[3] Exodus 32:19b.

[4] Not a <u>real</u> quote—see Exodus 34:1-4.
[5] Exodus 34:1b.

WAS THAT SECOND SET OF TABLES AN "ORIGINAL AUTOGRAPH?"

Nope. But was it <u>still</u> the <u>exact</u> <u>words</u> <u>of</u> <u>God</u>?

—Of course!

THERE IS <u>NO</u> "ORIGINAL AUTOGRAPH" OF THE TEN COMMANDMENTS. <u>ONLY</u> A <u>PERFECT</u> <u>COPY</u>.

WHAT HAPPENED TO THE SECOND SET?

God had Moses make a special box, called "the ark of the covenant." He told Moses to put that <u>copy</u> of the Ten Commandments into the ark, along with a jar of food from God that the people called *manna*[1] and his brother Aaron's rod (stick) that miraculously budded.[2]

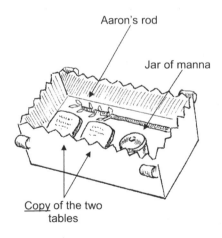

Aaron's rod

Jar of manna

Copy of the two tables

REMEMBER—

It's a **copy**, not an "original autograph," but it's <u>still</u> <u>God's</u> <u>exact</u> <u>words</u>.

God <u>didn't</u> make <u>any</u> <u>mistakes</u> on His **copy**!

---

[1] *Manna* literally means, "What <u>is</u> it?"
[2] See Deuteronomy 10:2-5; Exodus 16:33-34; Numbers 17:8-10; Hebrews 9:4.

ARE THOSE THE ONLY WORDS OF GOD?
No way!

God gave **603 other** commands to Moses as well. When God told Moses all this, he had to write it <u>somewhere</u>. Stones were too <u>heavy</u> and way too <u>cumbersome</u> to carry around. So Moses killed an animal, skinned it, prepared the animal's hide and made inks to write on it. It was made into one huge strip rolled up, with a stick at each end, to make a leather <u>scroll</u>.

It looked something like this.

The Sefer Torah

It was written, from right to left, in Hebrew. The whole scroll of the Law was called the *Torah*. Scroll is *sefer* in Hebrew, so the Torah Scroll is called: the "Sefer Torah."

Is that <u>all</u> the words of God? No—God had Moses write a journal of all the important stuff in his life, **plus** the 603 commands, **plus** a 2nd and 3rd <u>copy</u> of the Ten Commandments, **plus** all the main events from the Creation to the days of slavery in Egypt. **Whew!**

SO MOSES MADE FIVE "BOOKS" IN ONE SCROLL:
- **GENESIS** (Creation to Joseph in Egypt)
- **EXODUS** (Slavery in Egypt to building God's Tabernacle)
- **LEVITICUS** (Rules for Levite Priests)
- **NUMBERS** (The 40 years of wandering in the desert)
- **DEUTERONOMY** (Moses' speech to the Israelites before they entered Canaan)

GOOD THING MOSES HAD <u>40</u> YEARS TO WRITE ALL THIS!

What happened to that enormous scroll?

After Moses read his <u>long</u> <u>speech</u> (that we call Deuteronomy—"second giving of the Law" by Moses) to Israel, he took the huge scroll and handed it to the Levite priests, as a warning never to **break** or **change** God's laws. The priests put this book of the law in the side of the ark of the covenant of the LORD their God.[1] (But **not** before the last part of Deuteronomy was written!)[2]

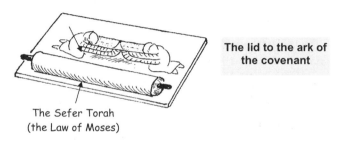

The lid to the ark of the covenant

The Sefer Torah
(the Law of Moses)

ALL <u>FIVE</u> <u>BOOKS</u> OF MOSES ARE **GOD'S WORDS**!

Did they just <u>leave</u> that one scroll <u>alone</u> in the side of the ark? Of course not. The Levites—who were in charge of God's words, so to speak—made copies of Moses' scroll. Would <u>you</u> want only <u>one</u> of an extremely valuable document? I hope not. What would you do if you ever <u>lost</u> it?

So the Levites painstakingly <u>copied</u> <u>every</u> <u>letter</u> of Moses' five books, for safe keeping. Wouldn't you?

---

[1] See Deuteronomy 31:24-27.
[2] Deuteronomy 34,which records Moses' death, written by Joshua or a priest.

GOD DIDN'T WANT THE "ORIGINAL AUTOGRAPHS" <u>HIDDEN</u>— HE WANTED THEM PERFECTLY <u>COPIED</u>.

God set the example—<u>He</u> <u>knew</u> Moses would break the 1st set of the Ten Commandments. After all, <u>He</u> <u>is</u> <u>God</u>! So **God Himself** showed us what He wants us to do!

GOD PERFECTLY COPIED HIS WORDS
ON THE 2ND SET OF TABLES,
BECAUSE **HE WANTS <u>US</u> TO MAKE
PERFECT COPIES** OF HIS WORDS, TOO.

How many exact copies did the Levitical priests make? Lots and lots. They *had* to. Why? Because scrolls made of leather don't exist forever—not if they are read over and over, with fingers touching the words, oils in the hands, time and weather aging them more and more.

So any thinking Levite would make a MASTER COPY, then use *that* to make all *other* copies.

Then when the MASTER COPY fell apart, a *backup* would be the <u>new</u> MASTER COPY, and so on.

DID THE LEVITES MAKE MISTAKES?
ARE YOU KIDDING?
THEY WERE <u>SCARED</u> <u>TO</u> <u>DEATH</u>
TO CHANGE <u>ONE</u> <u>LETTER</u> OF GOD'S WORDS!

The Hebrews were very <u>careful</u> about how they copied God's words. In the 1st century AD, the Jewish historian Josephus wrote:

> "We have given practical proof of our reverence for our own Scriptures. For although such long ages have now passed, **no one has ventured either to add, or to remove, or to alter a syllable**; and it is an instinct with every Jew, from the day of his birth, to regard them as the decrees of God, to abide by them, and, if need be, cheerfully to die for them."[1]

Is it an <u>exact</u> <u>duplicate</u> of the **master copy**?

No, sir. But I'm **almost** finished. Please, it's just **<u>one</u>** mistake!

You <u>must</u> **trash** the scroll and **start over**. <u>Every</u> <u>letter</u> must <u>be</u> <u>perfect.</u>

---

[1] Josephus, *Against Apion*, Book I, Section 8.

> **Levite priests copied Moses' scroll (or a master copy):**
> * Whenever they made a new MASTER COPY
> * Whenever one of the kings of Israel made his *required personal copy* of the Law[1]

God gave these instructions to each new king:

> "And it shall be, when he sitteth upon the throne of his kingdom, that **he shall write him a copy of this law in a book out of that which is before the priests**:

> And **it shall be with him**, and he shall read therein **all the days of his life**: that he may learn to fear the LORD his God, to keep all the words of this law and these statutes, to do them …"[2]

So when David said,

> "Thy word have I hid in mine heart, that I might not sin against thee,"[3]

He meant his *very own copy* of God's words, that he wrote down **with his own hands**!

---

[1] Many (not all) kings of Judah did this, certainly including David, Solomon, Jehoshaphat, Hezekiah, Joash & Josiah.
[2] Deuteronomy 17:18-19.
[3] Psalm 119:11.

ARE THOSE <u>ALL</u> OF GOD'S WORDS?
NOT AT ALL!

The books
of Moses

First God gave the **TORAH, (five books of Moses)**. After Moses' death in 1406 BC, God made **Joshua** the leader of God's people. His exploits are written down in the book of **Joshua** (from 1406 to about 1380 BC).

Joshua

Samson—one
of the Judges

Despite his <u>mostly</u> successful conquest of Canaan, the people fell into sin. Then God raised up judges (about 1380-1050 BC) to free the people when they repented. That's recorded in the book of **Judges**.

Here are some *other* HISTORY BOOKS
that God wanted written:

Ruth

Ruth (1300s BC) - This is the love story of how Boaz, the son of Rahab the harlot, met and married Ruth of Moab. God blessed them. They became the great-grandparents of King David!

1 Samuel—This is the first of a 6-book series (1 & 2 Samuel, 1 & 2 Kings, 1 & 2 Chronicles), which covers history from the prophet Samuel's birth to the fall of both the Northern and Southern Kingdoms in "Israel" (formerly called "Canaan"). Since the **1st** book covers Samuel's life (among other things), it is known as **"<u>First</u>" Samuel** (about 1105—1010 BC).

Samuel

These tell the HISTORY of the Kings of Israel:
1 & 2 Samuel, 1 & 2 Kings and 1 & 2 Chronicles

1 Samuel tells the story of King **Saul**, the <u>popular</u> 1ˢᵗ king of Israel who later refused to obey the LORD. Then God had Samuel anoint <u>David</u> king. King Saul spent years chasing David (the warrior youth who slew Goliath), to kill him. But Saul died and God protected David. **You *know* what happened next.**

Of course! **David became king!** King David reigned from 1010—970 BC. Read this in **2 Samuel and 1 Chronicles.**

The Bible is very <u>honest</u>. It not only records their victories, but also their <u>failures</u>.[1] **Solomon** reigned from 970—930 BC. He built the Temple to God, but also fell into idolatry with his 700 wives and 300 concubines! After Solomon died, the kingdom split. Ten tribes went to the north, and only Judah & Benjamin were left in the south, with Jerusalem as their capitol.

The idolatrous Northern Kingdom lasted from 930-722 BC till it fell to Assyria. The Southern Kingdom lasted till 605 BC and was a political puppet to Babylon till it fell to the Babylonians in 586 BC.

This history is told in **1 & 2 Kings and 2 Chronicles**.

---

[1] David's sin is recorded in 2 Samuel 11. Solomon's sin is in 1 Kings 11. Every <u>other</u> king's failure is also clearly described. Read about *any* king ... you'll see!

**The Israelites were slaves in Babylon for 70 years.
What about the <u>rest</u> of their HISTORY?**

Esther takes us to the years 483—473 BC.

It tells us how God preserved His people by making a young Jewish orphan the queen of Persia. The wicked Haman (who tried to get the Jews killed) ends up getting hanged on his own gallows!

Ezra starts at the decree of King Cyrus of Persia[1] in 538 BC for the Jews to rebuild their Temple. (They completed it in 516.) Then it tells how **Ezra** the priest went to Jerusalem (after the events in **Esther** took place) in 458-457 to teach holiness to the people and dedicate them to the LORD.

The Temple rebuilt:
Ezra and holiness

Nehemiah is a story of faith and courage. In 445 BC Nehemiah was cupbearer to the king *after* **Esther's** husband. God used him to get permission to fix the wall of Jerusalem. Despite opposition, it was done in just 52 days! Then **Ezra** taught them the Law and preached revival. And **Nehemiah** pushed through <u>major</u> reforms, to bring *repentance* and *holiness* among the priests. <u>It</u> <u>worked</u>!

Scriptures & the wall:
Rebuilding by Nehemiah

THEN GOD WAS SILENT FOR <u>400</u> <u>YEARS</u>.

---

[1] See 2 Chronicles 35:22-23 and Ezra chapter 1. Ezra starts *right after* 2 Chronicles!

GOD ALSO GAVE US "WRITINGS"[1]

The first book of "The Writings" is **Job**. Job lived after the Great Flood in Noah's day (2458 BC) covered the world. Way back in those days people lived longer. Job lived to see his great-great-grandkids!

Job was a rich man with a huge family. Then God let Satan take it all away and afflict him with boils. Job's three "friends" and the young Elihu try to explain why. Then God comes in and *really* sets him straight!

Psalms are the God-fearing poems of King **David** and other people, set to music, to be played by a stringed instrument.[2]

King **Solomon** and a few others wrote **Proverbs**. They are words of wisdom, just as true for us today as they were then.

The theme of **Ecclesiastes**: "All is vanity!"[3] That is what **Solomon** tells us. And he should know. He was not only **wise**; he was **filthy rich**!

The Song of Solomon is his wedding song to one of his 700 brides. It's beautiful, and is likened to God's love for His people.

---

[1] Jesus called them "The Psalms" in Luke 24:44.
[2] The Greek word for psalm, *psallo*, means "to pluck" a stringed instrument.
[3] "Vanity" means empty, unsatisfying, or unable to fulfill your desire.

Most of "The Writings" are <u>WISDOM LITERATURE</u>[1].

They answer the question, "What is wisdom?"

THE FEAR OF THE LORD[2]
IS THE BEGINNING OF WISDOM

And unto man he said,
Behold, **the fear of the Lord, that is wisdom**...
(Job 28:28)

The fear of the LORD is the beginning of wisdom ...
(Psalms 111:10)

The fear of the LORD is the beginning of wisdom:
and the knowledge of the holy is understanding ...
(Proverbs 9:10)

Let us hear the conclusion of the whole matter:
Fear God, and keep his commandments:
for this is **the whole duty of man**.
(Ecclesiastes 12:13)

"Fear God"
This is the most **important** teaching
of Wisdom Literature.

**IF YOU FEAR GOD,
YOU WILL BELIEVE HIS <u>EVERY</u> <u>WORD</u>.**

---

[1] The Song of Solomon is the *only* book in the Writings that doesn't contain this important truth. That's because it's a *romance*, not a book on doctrine.
[2] "Fear" is deep awe, reverence and respect for God. It includes *fearing* his judgment.

You can identify:
- The **Torah** (Genesis—Deuteronomy)
- The rest of the **history** (Joshua—Esther)

Those are called the **History Books**, or simply "**The Law**."

I've got it!

This makes sense.

You also recognize:
- The **Wisdom Literature** (Job—Ecclesiastes)
- The Song of Solomon

Those are called "**The Writings**," or by Jesus, "**The Psalms**."

The third category of the Old Testament is **The Prophets**. They divide into 2 groups:
- The **Major Prophets** (5 books)
- The **Minor Prophets** (12 books)

See <u>who they were</u>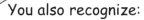
and <u>what they said</u> …

Now I'm curious.

Tell me about them!

The Four Major Prophets—and Five Books

Isaiah prophesied from 740-680 BC. He made 111 predictions, many of them about Jesus Christ, His birth, Godhead and Crucifixion.[1] He also told a **lot** about Israel and the End of the world.

Jeremiah is called "The Weeping Prophet." He preached from 627-580 BC without a <u>single</u> convert. Then God gave him a sad vision of what happened to Jerusalem when it fell in 586 BC.

That is recorded in poetic form in **Lamentations**.

Ezekiel saw visions from 592-570 BC, of God's presence removed from the Temple and of the evil activities of the priests. Yet God showed him <u>in detail</u> the exact specifications for the new Temple in the Millennium.[2] Those are recorded in chapters 40-48.

Daniel records happenings from 605 to 536 BC—long enough to be elevated by **3 rulers!** God granted him to know about the next **4 world kingdoms**—right up to the prophecies of **Revelation** and the 2nd Coming of Jesus! What a privilege!

---

[1] For instance, see Isaiah 7:14; chapter 11 and 52:13—53:12.

[2] "Millennium" means 1000 years when Jesus will rule the world after He returns. See

The remaining prophets are called "The Minor Prophets."

They were Minor in size, but not in <u>message</u>!

Hosea   Amos   Jonah Micah Habakkuk Haggai   Malachi
     Joel   Obadiah   Nahum Zephaniah Zechariah

They are called "Minor Prophets" because their books are way **shorter** than the Major Prophets. They were small enough to be written as a set of 12 **on one single scroll.** You got <u>12</u> prophets for the price of *one*!

Hosea—Prophesied 755-710 BC. God had him marry an adulterous woman to show what Israel was like. Then he took her back, like God accepts <u>us</u> when *we* repent.

Joel—Prophesied 835 BC. God gave Joel a vision of a locust attack, to compare it to God's judgment of the world. He also prophesied Pentecost.[1]

Amos—Prophesied 760-753 BC. God showed him the judgment of nations around Israel—and Israel herself!

Obadiah—Prophesied 840 BC. He foretold that pagan Edom would be judged, but that God would deliver Jerusalem.

---

[1] When God gave the Holy Ghost to Christians. See Joel 2:28-32 and Acts 2.

Jonah—Prophesied 760 BC. You cannot run away from God—or from His call. Jonah tried, and God used a huge fish to take him back to "Square One." Then Jonah prophesied doom to the people of Nineveh. But God showed them mercy.

Micah—Prophesied 742-703 BC. He and Isaiah foretold God exalting Jerusalem in the Last Days.

 Nahum—Prophesied 650 BC. Nineveh again fell into sin, so Nahum prophesied God's judgment on them.

Habakkuk—Prophesied 607 BC. Habakkuk asked God specific questions about His righteousness in punishing nations. Read what God said back to him!

 Zephaniah—Prophesied 640-632 BC. God showed him the judgment of Jerusalem and all nations, and the hope for Israel's future in the Last Days.

Haggai—Prophesied 520 BC to the returnees from Babylon. God wants His Temple rebuilt and will bless it—though it's not as beautiful as Solomon's.

 Zechariah—Prophesied 520-475 BC. He and Haggai prophesied about the Temple. But also God gave Zechariah many visions about the Last Days.

Malachi—Prophesied 433 BC to people who sinned greatly after Nehemiah returned to Babylon. He also foretold the coming of John the Baptist!

What about the <u>NEW</u> Testament?

- God used 8 men to write the New Testament books.
- The Gospels of Matthew, Mark, Luke & John are called by the names of the men who wrote them.
- Each New Testament book is named after
    - 1) the person or place it's addressed to,[1]
    - 2) the person who wrote it,[2] or
    - 3) the subject of the book.[3]

 **Matthew Levi** —Wrote the **Gospel of Matthew**. He was a "publican" (tax collector) until Jesus called him to follow Him.

John Mark—Wrote the **Gospel of Mark**. He once fled from a mission with Paul. But after Barnabas took him in, he became very useful.[4]

 **Luke**—Wrote the **Gospel of Luke** and **Acts of the Apostles**. He was Paul's "beloved physician"[5] who followed with him on many missionary journeys. He carefully researched Jesus' life, interviewing Mary, Elizabeth and many others.

---

[1] These are all Paul's books: Romans, 1 & 2 Corinthians, Galatians, Ephesians, Philippians, Colossians, 1 & 2 Thessalonians, 1 & 2 Timothy, Titus, Philemon and Hebrews.
[2] Matthew, Mark, Luke, John, James, 1 & 2 Peter, 1, 2 & 3 John and Jude
[3] The Acts of the Apostles and The Revelation of Jesus Christ.
[4] See Acts 13:1-13; 15:36-39; 2 Timothy 4:11.
[5] See Colossians 4:14

John—Wrote the **Gospel of John, 1, 2 & 3 John and The Revelation of Jesus Christ.** He was called "the beloved apostle," and it was thought he would never die. That was not true. But he *did* live a long time—till almost 100 AD!

Paul (Saul)—Wrote **14 books!** He first persecuted the church,[1] but then gave his whole heart and life to the Gospel. Paul wrote to ministers or churches he visited, to encourage them, teach their people and to correct their errors.

James & Jude —Wrote the books **James & Jude.** They were Jesus' 1/2 brothers.[2] James led the Jerusalem church. The book of **Jude** is a lot like **2 Peter.**

Simon Peter—Told John Mark many details for the **Gospel of Mark.** Peter wrote 1 & 2 Peter. He made mistakes in his life, but God used him to open the Gospel to the Gentiles — even though he didn't **want** to at first!

BY 100 AD THE WHOLE BIBLE WAS FINISHED. THE CATHOLIC "CHURCH" WAS STILL <u>300 YEARS</u> AWAY.

But look at what happened to God's words ...

[1] See Acts 8-9
[2] Mary and Joseph had James, Joses, Simon and Judas, but God is Jesus' Father, not Joseph (Matthew 13:55).

Chapter Two:
The Northern & Southern Streams—
Antioch and Alexandria

WHAT HAPPENED TO THE BIBLE AFTER 100 AD?

The Old Testament was accepted as one Book. And though the New Testament letters and Gospels were only recently written, churches traded and copied them. And these scrolls were all gathered together in one important city: **Antioch of Syria.**

Antioch was 310 miles **north** of Jerusalem. From there came the first Gospel missionary movement.

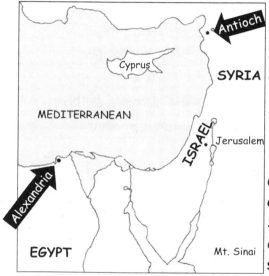

The Bible tells us that "the disciples were called Christians *first* in Antioch."[1] These Christian believers **collected** the holy scriptures and made many **copies** of them. Soon they were all collected into a **single Bible**.

The <u>Northern Stream</u> was God's preserved words in <u>Greek</u>.

But there was **another** city, 317 miles **southwest** of Jerusalem: **Alexandria, Egypt.** And in that city the "intellectuals" <u>perverted</u> the words of God.

HERE'S HOW IT HAPPENED …

[1] Acts 11:26.

IMPORTANT FACT: <u>EVERYONE</u> SPOKE GREEK.

From loosely 300 BC to 300 AD, **Greek** was the **"trade language"** people used to communicate all over the Roman Empire.

It was also the language of **philosophy**. That means every person who thought he was smart would read the Greek Philosophy of Socrates, Plato, Aristotle, Stoicism or Epicureanism. These *philosophers* all wanted to be "scholars." And guess what city turned out to be a philosopher's paradise? That's right! **Alexandria, Egypt!**

WHAT WERE "SCHOLARS" LIKE IN ALEXANDRIA?

Alexandria had a feeling and a character all its own. Author H.G. Wells wrote:

> **"Wisdom passed away from Alexandria** ... For the use of books was substituted **the worship of books**. Very speedily the learned became **a specialized ... class** with **unpleasant characteristics** of its own .... a new type of human being; shy, eccentric, unpractical, incapable of essentials, strangely **fierce upon trivialities** of literary detail, **as bitterly jealous of the colleague within as of the unlearned without – the Scholarly Man**. ... He was a sort of by-product of the intellectual process of mankind."[1]

—In other words, the Alexandrian "scholars" were stuck up, selfish, jealous **hypocrites** who could *never* agree on *anything.*

HMM... SO GUESS WHAT KIND OF <u>BIBLE</u> THEY CAME UP WITH?

---

[1] H.G. Wells, *The Outline of History* (1920), p. 305, quoted in *Final Authority* by Dr. William Grady (1993), p.77. Available from Chick Publications.

THE "BRILLIANT SCHOLARS" OF ALEXANDRIA:

You can already **imagine** what happened. **"Scholars"** from **Alexandria** got hold of the **pure Bible** of **Antioch**:

WHEN THE ALEXANDRIAN "SCHOLARS" GOT HOLD OF THE BIBLE, <u>EVERYTHING</u> CHANGED.

They argued like this for years in Alexandria. But the **main source** of the **false** Bible (as we know it today) was one particular "scholar" named **Origen**.

YES, ORIGEN WAS THE "ORIGIN!"

ORIGEN DIDN'T <u>LIKE</u> GOD'S PRESERVED BIBLE.

Why? Because he was a "scholar," of course!
During his life he wrote over 2,000 books[1], all infected
with his Greek philosophy. They are also filled with his
way of interpreting the Bible— "Allegorical Exegesis."

> **Main Point of Origen's "Allegorical Exegesis:"**
> <u>GOD</u> DIDN'T REALLY <u>MEAN</u> WHAT HE <u>SAID</u>!

Origen was <u>not</u> a Bible-believer.

- Origen *didn't* believe in the Old Testament miracles.
- Origen *didn't* believe many of Jesus' words or stories.
- Origen *didn't* believe the Holy Spirit was eternal.
- Origen *didn't* believe that **Jesus Christ is Almighty God!**[2]

But Origen was <u>tricky</u>—a **master** at playing <u>both sides</u>.

---

[1] Origen's friend Pamphilius said he wrote 6,000 books—though he might have exaggerated. But it's clear from history that Origen wrote *at least* 2,000.
[2] See Grady, *Final Authority*, pp. 191-195. See also Appendix A.

ORIGEN MADE UP A STRANGE GREEK BIBLE.

He pasted together his own **Greek Old Testament,** mixed with some old folk tales called the **Apocrypha,**[1] and added on **his own perverted New Testament.**

To dress up his Bible, he inserted New Testament verses into Old Testament passages.

> Origen .. <u>Look</u> at what Paul said in Romans 3! Can we drop it into Psalm 14?[2]

> Why not? They'll just think Paul quoted **my** Greek Old Testament!

It had to **look** like the Apostles and Jesus quoted **his Old Testament**. That made his book look "ancient," and gave it "authority." But he **added other books,** too.

> How's the Apocrypha coming? I want it **added** throughout.

> They'll love them, Origen. All those folk tales … pretty wild stuff!

> Good! They're not any more <u>true</u> than the **rest** of the Bible, anyway.

Satan used unbelieving Origen to make the first <u>counterfeit</u> Bible, **adding** and **removing** what he wanted.

---

[1] They became counterfeit "holy books."
[2] They tacked Romans 3:13-18 onto Psalm 14:3, adding **6 verses, 49 extra words!**

WHY DID ORIGEN WANT A GREEK BIBLE?

Why is **your** text in **Greek**?

Because the **Hebrew** tongue is **beneath** us, you *fool!*

Well, er, ... Actually, Origen didn't KNOW Hebrew well.[1]

And Greek is WAY EASIER to learn than Hebrew!

THE MYTH OF THE "ANCIENT SEPTUAGINT:"

Watch this! When I put **my Old Testament** and the **Apocrypha** together, guess what I'll **call** them?

What, O **Great One?**

CLAP!

CLAP!

I'll say they're the "**ancient**" Septuagint!

BRILLIANT!!

Origen gave the world **his** Bible, **not God's:**

Modified **Old Testament**
+ Folk tales called **Apocrypha**
+ Perverted **New Testament**
———————————————
= Origen's Alexandrian "Bible"

GREEK ONLY

Origen's Bible will play a **BIG part** in the 19th, 20th and 21st centuries.

---

[1] See Rev. J. Tixeront, *A Handbook of Patrology,* translated by S.A. Raemers (English Edition, 1920), p. 90

Origen lived an unusual life. At 18 he was made head teacher at the school of Alexandria. He taught from 204-230, *when he was kicked out*. He moved to Caesarea and was caught in the Decian persecution of 250 and **tortured.** After he was released, in **254 AD** he finally **died** of his wounds.

ORIGEN

For centuries he was **much too heretical** to be counted as a "Church Father." But times change!

As you will find out, nowadays Origen is treated like a "**saint**," and his writings are honored, not only by Roman Catholics, but by **Protestants** as well! And yet ... **he wasn't** a real **Christian**!!

WHAT HAPPENED TO ORIGEN'S BIBLE AFTER HE DIED?

- His counterfeit Bible was copied by other "scholars."[1]
- In the 300s they were asked to make **50 Bibles** (see chapter 4)
- The "scholars" at Alexandria wrote these 3 Bible perversions:
  - **Sinaiticus (about 350 AD)**
  - **Vaticanus (before 400 AD)**
  - **Alexandrinus (about 450 AD)**
- Those "scholarly" Bibles **disagree** over **3,000 times,** *in the 4 Gospels alone!!* They are what you call "false witnesses."

---

[1] Origen thought *his* Old Testament + Apocrypha (the "Septuagint") was *perfect - better than the Hebrew*. See Tixeront, *Handbook of Patrology*, p. 92.

SO NOW WE HAVE <u>TWO</u> <u>STREAMS</u>:
THE **NORTHERN** STREAM
AND THE **SOUTHERN** STREAM

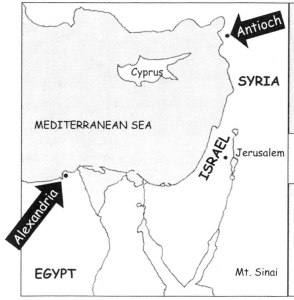

The Northern Stream was God's words <u>preserved</u> in Antioch of Syria.

The Southern Stream was God's words <u>perverted</u> in Alexandria, Egypt.

Was GOD surprised by the devil's counterfeit?
Of <u>course</u> not! The Lord knows <u>everything</u>.

And He had planned, before He made the universe,
to spread <u>His</u> <u>Bible</u> all over the world.

THE DEVIL <u>DIDN'T</u> <u>KNOW</u> <u>IT</u>,

But *behind the curtain* was a <u>new</u> world language:

LATIN!

In a valley of the Alps was a people that God used to translate His preserved words into Latin.

THESE PEOPLE WERE CALLED THE "VAUDOIS."

They lived in the Piedmont[1] Valleys of the Alps, at the northwest corner of Italy, east of France.[2] In about 120 AD some got saved, and went to **Antioch** to receive God's words.

Europe

THE VAUDOIS*

*Pronounced: vahd—WAH

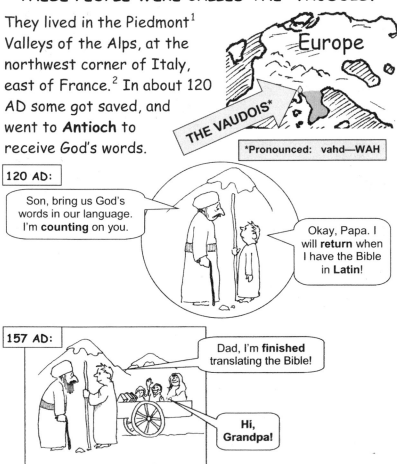

120 AD:

Son, bring us God's words in our language. I'm **counting** on you.

Okay, Papa. I will **return** when I have the Bible in **Latin**!

157 AD:

Dad, I'm **finished** translating the Bible!

Hi, **Grandpa!**

---

[1] Piedmont means "foot of the mountain." It was surrounded by mountains on three sides.
[2] This area where the Vaudois lived is also called the *Itala*.

AT LAST THE OLD LATIN BIBLE WAS FINISHED!

We call it "Old Latin" - but it wasn't old **then**! For a few hundred years, it was the world language. And now God's words were available to the whole Roman empire. Amazingly, it spread all the way to England before 200 AD.[1]

The Old Latin Bible spread so wide, Christians

called it the **Vulgate** (common) Bible. And Vaudois missionaries spread God's words, even down to Rome, two by two. They risked death—but the **Gospel** was more important than their **lives**.

The Roman emperors persecuted the early church.

I found **another** Bible!

Burn it!

This slaughter continued until Constantine was emperor.

---

[1] See *In Awe of Thy Word* by Gail Riplinger (2003), pp. 676—677. The basis for the Saxon (English) Bible was God's preserved Old Latin, not the later Catholic perversion by Jerome. (See chapter 4.)

Chapter Three:
The Caesars Change Costumes

WHO WAS CONSTANTINE?

Constantine was a **pagan**, just like most Romans were.

He worshipped the sun god, SOL INVICTUS, which means the **"unconquered sun"**.[1] If you were the devil and wanted this guy to obey you, what would you do? Use his devotion to the **sun god**, of course! And that is <u>exactly</u> what the devil did!

When his **dad**, Constantius Chlorus, died in 306 AD, his son Constantine didn't **automatically** or **officially** become an emperor. So in 312 AD, Constantine was battling his rival Maxentius (son of Maximian, a **previous** emperor) for the throne. Finally, at Milvian Bridge Constantine asked **his sun god** for a sign.

Constantine sees the ankh

Suddenly, he saw an **ankh**[2] in the sky and the words, *EN HOC SIGNO VINCES* ("**in this sign conquer**"). And Satan's forces made **sure** that he won.

The devil's plan for Rome, "MYSTERY BABYLON THE GREAT,"[3] was taking shape.

---

[1] See *Introduction to the History of Christianity*, edited by Tim Dowley (1990), pp. 139-140. Also see *The Force* (Crusader Comic # 15, p. 20), available from Chick Publications.
[2] See Crusader comics *The Force*, p. 20 and *Sabotage?* pp. 19-20.
[3] See Revelation 17:5.

The Emperor of Rome
had a number of important titles.

My lord, as our new Caesar, we present you with the title, **Pontifex Maximus**.

That will fit my plans **nicely**.

Constantine was **pleased**.
The Pontifex Maximus was a **powerful person**.

WHAT IS A "PONTIFEX MAXIMUS"?

In Greek and Roman religion was a god called **Neptune** (Poseidon in Greek). According to their myths Neptune lived and ruled the oceans from under the sea.

The one who ruled Neptune was called the "chief bridge builder," or **Pontifex Maximus**. He had power over the waters—even over Neptune himself. And soon he regulated **other** religions as well.

Each of his priests was called a **Pontifex**.

The Pontifex Maximus had great **power** over the pagans of the Roman Empire:

- He set the Roman calendar
- He set the holidays
- He set the sacrifices to the gods

That way Constantine could hold tight control over the pagan religions.

But he also made himself the head of the "church"!

Your **highness**, we have brought what you **commanded**.

Good! Now **all** shall know me as the **Bishop of Bishops**!

SO AS "BISHOP OF BISHOPS" HE PROCLAIMED:

Christianity is **legal!**

Now it was politically correct to be "converted"...

Now **we're** saved **too**, right? (Hic!)

Haw haw! Why **not**? I'll drink to **that**!

313 AD: Edict of Milan

FALSE CONVERSIONS WERE EVERYWHERE.

Eusebius of Caesarea (263-339) was Constantine's **lap-dog**. He treated his emperor like he was a **god**. And **anything** that Constantine **wanted**, Eusebius was there to **get it** for him.

One day Constantine called upon his obedient servant:

CONSTANTINE WANTED ONLY ONE "CHURCH."

But the empire was filled with **pagans**. So he decided to "**Christianize**" them, whether they **wanted** it or **not!**

The answer is **simple**: we'll give all the old gods "**Christian**" names!

My lord, you are a **genius!**

I know.

Now he wanted to **UNITE these so-called "Christians."**
So in 325 AD, Constantine as **Bishop of Bishops** presided over the Council of Nicea—attended by over 250 bishops.[1] It was to decide whose doctrine of the Godhead would be followed.

"Stop the religious arguments. We must all try to get along."

The emperor's plan **worked**. The council finally stopped bickering. Now he was free to put his **other** plans into action.

---

[1] Eusebius said 250, but Athanasius said 318 bishops were at the Council.

CONSTANTINE WANTED A CITY OF HIS OWN.

But could he change the name of **Rome**? Of **course** not! So in 330 AD he and a **great entourage** packed up and **left**.

They moved to **Byzantium**, NW of modern Turkey.

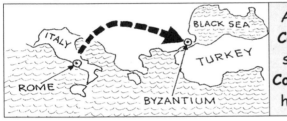

And what would **Constantine**, the son of emperor **Constantius**, name his new **capitol**?

What else? CONSTANTINOPLE!

Now, quick guess: **What** did he name his **three sons**?

Who else?

Constantius II, Constantine II and **Constans!**

Constantine **couldn't be a narcissist,** could he?

THE BISHOP OF ROME BECAME A RICH MAN!

Constantine left behind for the bishop a huge **palace**, other **properties** and lots of **wealth**. In **321 AD** this last great Caesar had made "the venerable day of the sun" (Sunday) into a "Christian" holy day. He also had ordered a **basilica** (a reformed pagan temple) to be built on the hill **Vaticanus**. The **Roman Catholic religion** was forming. And the <u>wealth</u> <u>of</u> <u>Rome</u> was right at the bishop's fingertips. **Everything was falling into place.**

But in **337** Constantine died, and his **three brat kids** fought each other for the throne. **Constantine's kingdom fell apart** while the **bishop's kingdom grew!**

- **340: Constantine II** was murdered by Constans
- **350: Constans** was murdered by his own servants
- **361: Constantius II** died
- …   And then it got **worse**.

THE POWER OF THE CAESARS WENT TO <u>ROME</u>.

Chapter Four:
The Beginning
of the Roman "Church"

ROMAN CATHOLICISM WAS FORMED
IN JUST <u>ONE</u> <u>CENTURY</u>.

Siricius (384-399) was the **first** Roman Bishop to call himself "**Pontifex Maximus**" and a **new** term, "**Pope**" (papa). Now **pagan Rome** became the "holy" city. The pope had the religious powers of **Caesar** and claimed to **rule** the "church."

But he needed the people to be fully under his control. The **Vaudois** and others across the empire had God's words preserved in their **Old Latin Bible**. They **knew** that Rome was the "whore of Babylon"[2] and **revealed** the devil's scheme. So Satan went on the warpath. And one day the pope declared:

"WE NEED OUR <u>OWN</u> BIBLE!"

Satan had the <u>perfect</u> man: a monk named JEROME.

[1] See *The History of the New Testament Church* by Dr. Peter S. Ruckman (1982), Vol. 1, pp. 153-4.
[2] See Revelation 17-18 and 2 Thessalonians 2:3-6. Also see *A Woman Rides the Beast* by Dave Hunt (1994), available from Chick Publications.

Jerome (340-420) **was another intellectual like Origen.** In fact, **his first books** (379-381) were simply his **Latin translations** of Origen's writings.

From **382-390** Jerome worked on his **rewrite** of the true Old Latin Bible. (Jerome **rejected** God's preserved **Old Latin.**) At

first he just translated his Latin Bible from **Origen's Greek counterfeit**—the so-called "Septuagint."

Jerome spent from 382-385 writing in **Rome**, but was so **conceited** that he made a **lot** of enemies. So he moved to **Bethlehem** and studied with Jewish rabbis. As soon as he learned a little Hebrew, Jerome began **changing** a few of Origen's words! People believed the so-called "Septuagint" was *purer* than the Hebrew, so Jerome was in **hot water** again.

Please?

NO!!

That's when a young **intellectual** named **Augustine** of Hippo (354-430) wrote letters to Jerome, **begging** the "most esteemed" scholar to switch **back** to the Septuagint.

HE REFUSED!

BY 405 AD,
JEROME FINISHED HIS LATIN PERVERSION.

This is how he put together **his** so-called "**Bible:**"

- The **true** Old Latin Bible was so well-known and **popular** (Christians called it the *Vulgate*—the "common" Bible) that he had to leave the **well-known** Old Latin verses **as they were.**

- A **lot** of his Bible was like **Origen's "Septuagint" perversion.** But he **still** changed **certain** words to read like **his** own "scholarly interpretation" of the Hebrew. He was an **intellectual** to the end!

- The <u>final</u> insult was the **name** of Jerome's disaster: They called it the "Roman Catholic **LATIN VULGATE!!**"

The pope expected their **new** "Vulgate" would **catch on** right away with faithful "Catholics." But **too many people** knew God's **genuine** words to be fooled by this <u>counterfeit.</u>

WHAT? They <u>still</u> use the Old Latin?

Let's just say the pope <u>wasn't</u> too happy about this.

I'll **kill them all** and then I'll destroy their **Bibles!**

The popes would have loved to extinguish all true Christians. But they were **interrupted** in 410 by an invasion of **Visigoths**.

For the first time in 800 years Rome was invaded.

It wasn't very pretty.

Over the **next decades**, Rome was repeatedly **attacked** and **plundered**. Finally the Roman government **collapsed**.

—And the **only thing left** to pick up the pieces was that pagan, perverted, Pontifex-led, priest-filled **Roman Catholic "church!"**

Catholic Rome got the reins of government and began destroying God's words in Old Latin, but **nothing** takes **GOD** by surprise! Faithful believers **hid** their Bibles.

Son, **remember** this place.

Okay, Dad.

But this was <u>only</u> the **beginning**. Counterfeit Christianity was about to take shape.

First, **Augustine wrote** *The City of God* (413-426) claiming **that the Roman Catholic religion is of** God!

Here are some other lies Augustine claimed:

- Roman Catholics are the "true," "spiritual" **Israel**.
- God's promises to Israel are only fulfilled in the "church," not the literal **Israel**.
- The "true" **Greek Bible** is Origen's Septuagint.
- Jerome wrote the "true" **Latin Bible**.

Second, **pope Celestine I (422-432 AD) turned a "goddess" into Mary!**

- He was a friend of Augustine's.
- He called the Council of Ephesus (431 AD).
- His Council now called Mary—**the "mother of God"** (Greek, *theotokos*).

The idol-makers were thrilled! They lost **none** of *their* business. They had once made statues of **Diana**, the Ephesian goddess (Acts 19:28-35). Now they made statues of **Mary**, supposedly "God's mother."

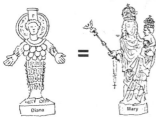

Now the Roman Catholic system had its own:

- Counterfeit **leader**—the pope
- Counterfeit **Mary** to worship
- Counterfeit **Jesus** wafer god
- Counterfeit **Vulgate Bible**

These Mary-worshipers were Catholics—not Christians!

And *third*,
A BIG LIE:

> **"To learn about 'true' early Christianity Read the Church Fathers"**

Warning:

The "Early Church Fathers" were not the *real* Early Church Fathers!

"Saint" Augustine   "Saint" Jerome   "Saint" Origen   "Saint" Eusebius   "Saint" Irenaeus

SURPRISE We're really "fathers" of Roman Catholicism!

If you want to be a **Roman Catholic**, read *their* books.

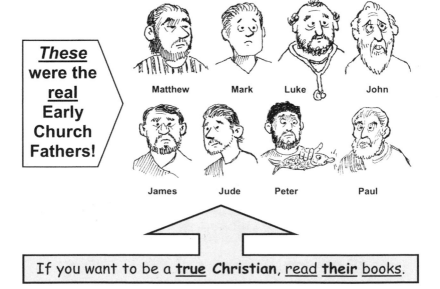

These were the **real** Early Church Fathers!

Matthew   Mark   Luke   John

James   Jude   Peter   Paul

If you want to be a **true** Christian, read **their** books.

THIS WAS THE BIGGEST CON JOB IN HISTORY!

Satan was **clever**. Only his **priests** were "qualified" to interpret Jerome's fake "Latin Vulgate Bible." None of

these Catholics had God's words. So they became **superstitious** and **religious**—in no way **Christian**. They were <u>deceived</u> by a phony Vulgate. So now the Catholic priests ruled over the people like little gods.

The popes made **everyone** worship the fake Mary — OR ELSE!

The Bible says Roman Catholicism is

"... the **great whore** that sitteth upon many waters: With whom the kings of the earth have committed fornication ..."
(Revelation 17:1-2)

Heh heh! That's my **boy**!

From Constantine to Celestine, **true** Christians were heading for the hills. Till now the Vaudois had been tucked safely inside the lower Alps.

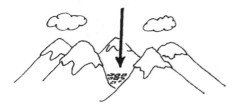

BUT <u>PERSECUTION</u> WAS ON ITS WAY!

THE POPE GAVE HIS ULTIMATUM.

The armies of the pope were **more than happy** to destroy the Bible believing Christians— **especially** since they could <u>keep</u> the property of those they killed!

Ignorance was rampant in Roman Catholic nations.

Even the **priests** were often **illiterate**, unable to read the counterfeit Bible, much less God's preserved words in Old Latin. **But among the Vaudois**, who still sent missionaries two by two across the world, God's holy words gave them purpose.

Mom! Dad! I just **memorized** the **Gospel of Mark**!

That's **great**! What are you going to do **now**?

Memorize the **Psalms of David**!

That's **our son**!

These missionaries were **always ready**[1] to share God's holy words.

We're **priests**, but we've never even **seen** a Bible ...

Their **Bibles** were carefully **hidden** inside their rough cloaks.[2]

Want to see one of **mine**?

Or should I just **quote** it for you?

Many Roman Catholics were converted by Vaudois. Even after **terrible persecutions**, the Vaudois stayed **faithful**. They **knew** one day their **faith** would **pay off**.

THIS CONTINUED THROUGH THE DARK AGES.

[1] See 1 Peter 3:15-17.
[2] See Wilkinson in *Which Bible?* edited by David Otis Fuller (1975), p. 212.

Chapter Five:

Light Shines in the Dark Ages

TRUE CHRISTIANS WERE KILLED OR IN HIDING.

It took **900 years** for the Catholics to destroy **most Old Latin Bibles** and kill their owners. Then God moved <u>one man</u> to translate God's words from Old Latin into English:

JOHN WYCLIFFE
(1320-84).

By **1380** he translated the New Testament, and by **1382** the complete English Bible. He is now honored for his work and called:

"The MORNING STAR of the REFORMATION."

Do you think the Catholic leaders would <u>let</u> a **non-Catholic** Latin Bible get put into common English? Of **course** not! As **soon** as Wycliffe died, soon-to-be Catholic **John Purvey** started **perverting** that Bible! Each year, Wycliffe's Bible was changed to look like an English version of a **Roman Catholic Vulgate!**

DID YOU KNOW:

- Back then it was **illegal** to translate the Bible?
- The **only** "legal" language of education was **LATIN**?
- You could **die**, simply for **not** being a Roman Catholic?
- Wycliffe was willing to *break* the Roman Catholic rules, simply because he **believed the Bible**?

BUT WYCLIFFE FEARED <u>GOD</u>, NOT THE <u>POPE</u>!

Wycliffe knew what really mattered in life.

God's **word** is the life of the world!

He **loved** God's words. He encouraged others to spread God's words **everywhere**. Catholics **hated** them, calling them "Lollards" (babblers).

Wycliffe was also a tract publisher.[1] (My kind of guy!)

What do you think of the latest tract?

OH, brother John — This is **HOT!**

They are going to **HATE** you for this!

Wycliffe was **fearless** when he attacked the "great whore"[2] in his tracts.

Do you realize all these things—Wycliffe's books, his tracts and his Bible—all were **hand-written?** There was still no printing press, and books were extremely **expensive** to make. But John **kept** writing, challenging and exposing the Roman Catholic system at **every** turn. **He never stopped to the day of his death!**

FINALLY WYCLIFFE DIED.
HE <u>COULDN'T</u> BE A THREAT **NOW** ...
COULD HE?

---

[1] For more information about Wycliffe, see Grady, *Final Authority* (1993), pp. 120-129, and Gail Riplinger, *In Awe of Thy Word* (2003), pp. 749-796.
[2] See Revelation 17:1.

You won't believe this! In 1415, 21 years after he died, his **body** was **taken out of the grave** and tried for **heresy**.

John Wycliffe, you are accused of **rebellion** against **Mother Church!**

What do you have to **say** for yourself?

After his "fair trial," Wycliffe was found to be guilty. (**Big surprise!**) They then burned up his body and poured his ashes into the Severn River.

"**There**! You don't scare **US** anymore!"

You have to realize what a **threat** it was to put God's words into the hands of the **people**. But for now it seemed their troubles were all over.

**BUT GOD WASN'T FINISHED!
HE WAS ABOUT TO RAISE UP
A FAITHFUL ROMAN CATHOLIC
TO CHANGE THE WORLD FOREVER ...**

JOHNNY GOOSEBUMPS!

(His **German** name was, "Johannes Gensfleisch," but **that's** what the name **meant**.) He eventually decided to **name** himself by that part of the **city of Mainz**, Germany, where his **family** lived. We know him as:

JOHANNES GUTENBERG

    Gutenberg (1398-1468) was an **inventor**. He tried to earn money by making Catholic trinkets. But he knew there was more money printing up letters of **Indulgence** (to reduce the time you burn in "Purgatory"[1]). The German Catholics were very **superstitious** and would pay **dearly** to keep out of Purgatory! So whoever could print Indulgences the fastest would be the richest, right? Gutenberg had a plan to get rich. And by **1450** he had **invented** the first movable-type **printing press**!

You must **swear** never to reveal the secret of my **printing press**!

I **swear**!

So do I!

Me **too**!

    In the 1450s he **also** published about **200** huge Roman Catholic Latin Vulgate Bibles. He printed more than **anyone else**, in only <u>5 years</u>, thanks to his **secret** —his **printing press**. But tell me: Could **you** could keep a secret **that big** for long?

---

[1] **Purgatory** is a mythological place to burn off your sins before you can go to heaven. And **Indulgences** were "God's permission" to spend less time in Purgatory. Indulgences are **fake** and **unnecessary** because Jesus **already** purged our sins. Read **Hebrews 1:3** in your KJV!

WHAT HAPPENED TO GUTENBERG'S "SECRET" ?

In those days two archbishops, **Diether** of Isenburg and **Adolph II** of Nassau, were warring over who would be the Arch-Chancellor of Germany and archbishop of Mainz. The **city** supported **Diether**. But the **pope** supported **Adolph II**. And on the night of October 28, 1462, Adolph II invaded Mainz, Germany.

THIS WAS **THE MOMENT** THE PRINTERS HAD BEEN **WAITING** FOR!

In all the disturbance, who would notice a number of **dark figures** sneaking out during the night? Of course, they were all carrying parts of the **printing presses**, but hey, it was dark!

Mainz is invaded by Adolph II

I'm **gone!**

So am **I!**

Me **too!**

Soon printing presses showed up in cities <u>all across</u> the "Holy Roman Empire." By **1500**, 133 editions of the Bible (Catholic) were published and a total of **15 million** books had been printed. **The "secret" was out!**

THE STAGE WAS SET ... NOW <u>GOD'S</u> WORDS WERE ABOUT TO SPREAD ACROSS THE GLOBE!

THE REFORMATION STARTED WITH A BOY

Just four years after the invasion of Mainz, **Desiderius Erasmus** (1466-1536) was born.[1] His father **copied documents** to make money. He even sent young Erasmus to a school that **copied manuscripts**—a great beginning. But soon his parents died. Erasmus inherited a **fortune**. And his new "guardians" wanted **all** of it!

Little boy, you should be in a **monastery**.

Listen to him! The "**Church**" will take care of your **fortune**.

Uh, okay.

Sucker!

In later years, Erasmus confessed:

I made a **terrible** mistake. I was **forced** to become a priest.

Young rich boys who became monks were **manipulated** into orgies, tortured and thrown into dungeons ... to **crush** them into submission!

And my fortune was **stolen** by the Roman Catholic "church."

Young Erasmus joined the monastery and **absorbed** its rich **libraries**. He read and copied their books (the way his father had). Now he carefully **avoided** taking the vows of a priest. But **about age 20** they forced him to choke out the words, like a prisoner who is tortured into making a false confession. He was **stuck!**

---

[1] Most of the information in this section comes from the excellent research of Gail Riplinger's *In Awe of Thy Word* (2003), Chapter 27, "The Life of Erasmus." See also *Answers to Your Bible Version Questions* (2003), pp. 43-46. Both books are available from Chick Publications.

BUT GOD HAD A PURPOSE TO ERASMUS' LIFE

None of this happened by **accident**. **God** chose Erasmus as His vessel to shine the light of His Gospel during the hellish Dark Ages. You know what? Erasmus was God's **undercover agent!**

By day he was a **faithful Roman Catholic**, serving the pope, working diligently in the libraries.

But at night he **wrote tracts** that **ridiculed** the Catholic system. (Another tract-publishing hero!)

This was a **dangerous** game. But Erasmus played it because he utterly **despised** the **devilish** pope. He continued devouring parish libraries, until he finally had his **opportunity**.

To study in other libraries, I should get a **Doctorate**.

Yet **Doctors** are the very ones that push **Catholic heresies!**

True, but Erasmus would finally be _free_ of the Catholic priesthood!

From 20 years old to his death, he **never** wore a monk's robe, lived in a monastery or exercised a **single** priestly function. He was free to study and write.

GOD HONORED ERASMUS' DEVOTION TO TRUTH

First, he <u>survived</u> <u>his</u> <u>education</u> at the hands of strict professors like those in the tiny college of Montaigu in the University of Paris. So he was free to visit libraries.

Second, he <u>moved</u> <u>to</u> <u>Italy</u> to see their **libraries** and compare **Bible manuscripts** and other books. God worked out the **timing** so he could devour these libraries before 1527, when Rome was sacked and the libraries were destroyed.

Third, having scoured Italy for manuscripts, he <u>spent</u> <u>the</u> <u>rest</u> <u>of</u> <u>his</u> <u>life</u> <u>in</u> <u>England</u> and northern Europe. It was time for him to publish a **true** Bible, not a false Catholic one.

Those are the words of God

But **this** Catholic Bible is a devilish **joke** .. and it's **Origen's** fault!

Christians need a **correct** Greek and Latin Bible, like **these** I have here.

Erasmus was so **brilliant** that he was honored by kings from all over, who wanted his advice. God put him in a **perfect position** to print God's words in Greek and Latin.

Erasmus, this is a request from **Henry VIII** in **England!**

He had only to <u>complete</u> his Greek-Latin New Testament ...

All his life Erasmus had read handwritten Bibles that were based on the **preserved Old Latin**. And now he had the opportunity to bring **God's words in Greek and Latin** to the printing press. But another, **faithful Catholic** had created a Bible out of the Roman Catholic Latin Vulgate. He was <u>ahead</u> of Erasmus. And if **he** got the pope's blessing, the **true** Bible would lose out.

How can I get the pope to endorse a **true Bible**?

I've **got** it! I'll **flatter** him on the Dedication page!

The **pope** read Erasmus' fake "**praise**." He was **thrilled**:

I **love** his new Bible ... he looks upon **me** as **God**! Print it **as it is**!

It worked! In 1516 the **genuine New Testament**, once known only in secret, was printed **openly**.

By the time they **figured out** what Erasmus had done, his **New Testament** had covered **Europe**. This was the Bible text that had **always** been received by **true** Christians. **That** is why a century later it was popularly known by believers as: **THE "RECEIVED TEXT" !!**

NOBODY KNEW IT EXCEPT GOD, BUT ...
THE <u>REFORMATION</u> WAS ALREADY BEGINNING!
GOD WAS BUSY PREPARING A YOUNG MONK ...

Chapter Six:
Reformation—and Revenge

1510: A young MARTIN LUTHER faced his superior.

Brother Martin, we are sending you to **Rome** to settle a **dispute** among our brothers.

Rome? The city of **God**? I'm so <u>unworthy!</u>

This was the **highlight** of his **life!** Martin would see the glories of Rome. He was **sure** his faith would be **renewed**. When Luther got to **Rome**, he cried:

Holy Rome, I **salute** thee!

Then he entered the "holy city" with tears of joy.

But <u>**what** he **saw**</u> put him into **shock!**

You're the one for me.

Come **here**, little **boy!**

If there is a **hell**, then Rome is **built** upon it!

A discouraged Martin Luther went back to his **duties,** though he was frustrated. But a few years later, the pope wanted money to build "Saint Peter's Basilica" at Vaticanus hill. And **one day** an Inquisition priest named **John Tetzel** came waltzing into Germany, raising **money** for the pope by selling **Indulgences.**

Put your **coin** in my coffer and you'll be **forgiven**—even if you **violated** the Holy **Virgin Mother** of God!

Wonderful! Give me **five!** I want my neighbor's **wife!**

Hey... me **too!**

Money poured into "coffers" (money boxes) from all over Europe. **Sin** was **for sale—cheap!** Superstitious and guilty Catholics **paid** to keep **out** of a mythological **Purgatory.** And Rome got enormously **rich!**

Luther lost it! He was **outraged.** And he wrote something that threatened to **topple** the entire Roman Catholic system. On October 31st, 1517[1], Luther nailed his "95 Theses" to the Wittenberg church door.

The **righteous** shall live by FAITH!

His words sparked a **fire** that triggered a huge **revolution.** Multitudes started **leaving** the "holy" Roman church in **disgust!**

---

[1] "Reformation Day." It was a momentous day, but now it's called "Halloween!"

Martin Luther (1483-1546) **had already** been reading **Erasmus'** Greek New Testament since **1516**. So he **knew** what God's preserved words said about salvation. And though there were numerous *hand-written* Bibles in German, he knew he must bring God's preserved words through the **printing press**.

1522: Martin Luther made his translation of the New Testament in only **11 weeks**.

It was dubbed the "September Testament."

1534: He **finished** the **Bible**[1]. It was similar to the "Tepl" Bible (a 1389 translation of the Old Latin[2] into German). **Germany** had become the <u>heart</u> of the Reformation.

THE TRUE BIBLE SPREAD LIKE WILDFIRE!

---

[1] See *The Reformation Era: 1500-1650* by Harold Grimm (1965), pp. 147, 229.
[2] See Gail Riplinger, *In Awe of Thy Word* (2003), Chapter 27, p. 977 .

GOD HAD <u>BIG</u> <u>PLANS</u> FOR ENGLAND.

Satan wanted that small island country for **himself**. He kept them in **darkness**. But God chose <u>one</u> <u>man</u> to bring **light** to England: **WILLIAM TYNDALE.**

William Tyndale (1494-1536) read God's preserved words in Greek. (Know how? **Erasmus** was Tyndale's **Greek teacher!**)
In 1523 Tyndale asked to translate them into English.

But he <u>didn't</u> get the answer he wanted.

TYNDALE KNEW WHERE TO GO FOR HELP.

I **KNOW** God wants me to do this.

He **had** to leave England. So he packed up his research and went to **Germany**.

We're at **war**, brother. You **must** translate the New Testament **here**.

In Wittenberg, Tyndale found a strong **ally** in **Martin Luther**.

And in **1525**, Tyndale published the first **preserved English New Testament**.

But William wasn't **only** an expert in **English**. **William Buschius**, a literary leader and friend of Erasmus, said that Tyndale:

> "… was so complete a master of **seven** languages – Hebrew, Greek, Latin, Italian, Spanish, English, French – that you would fancy that **whichever** he spoke in was his **native tongue**."[1]

Now even the boy who drives the **plow** will be able to read God's **words**!

But <u>how</u> will Tyndale get it <u>back</u> into England?

---

[1] See Gail Riplinger, *In Awe of Thy Word* (2003), pp. 866-867, and *Which Bible?* edited by David Otis Fuller (1975), pp. 228-229.

Now comes the tricky part. But God <u>always</u> has a way.

We'll **sneak** them into England by **boat**. Let's **pray** God will open their **hearts** and minds.

... And so he did. Night journeys were frequent, and the Bibles slipped by. **No one** noticed.

But the Catholic leaders had **other** plans for them, once they were in **England**. They actually **bought** the **Bibles!**

I want **every single one!**

Of course, but **all** of 'em, my lord?

Haw Haw! That's the **end** of **his** work!

That's what <u>you</u> think!

Look at the money! Now you can print even **better** Bibles!

And so even **burning** his Bibles helped Tyndale!

God worked out all things for His good.

GOD <u>had</u> a way!

TYNDALE WAS ON HIS ENEMIES' HIT LIST!

"Saint" Thomas More[1] (1478-1535), is honored by Catholics for his "godly fairness," politeness, sense of humor and intelligence.

But he had only **HATRED** for Martin Luther, Tyndale, and **anyone** who loved God's words! He **burned Bible-believers** at the stake and **tortured** them in his <u>own house</u>![2]

He paid **big bucks** to get <u>someone</u> to betray Tyndale. In our money, it would be like a "million dollar hit." The word was out: **FIND TYNDALE!**

That "someone" was Henry Phillips. No one knew <u>what</u> he was doing or <u>why</u>. But this **"Judas"** became Tyndale's buddy ... then **betrayed him!**

Henry! Wha...?

There he is! **ARREST HIM!**

---

[1] In 2000 pope John Paul II made this **anti-Protestant** "patron saint of statesmen and politicians." As a slap against Protestants, he did it on **Reformation Day**—October 31st! (See p. 72.)

[2] See *God's Bestseller* by Brian Moynahan (2002), pp. 205-266 and *In the Beginning* by Alister McGrath (2001), pp. 82-83. (Be warned: More wrote **dirty** words against Luther!). See also *Acts & Monuments*, by John Foxe (1583), Vol. IV, pp. 619-705.

TYNDALE SUFFERED IN PRISON FOR 16 MONTHS

Tyndale lay there in a cold, dark and damp cell. His clothing was **worn out**, and so was **he**. But **God answered** his prayers: he **won** the keeper and his daughter and others on the staff **for Christ!**

But on October 6, 1536, his time had run out.

... And God answered <u>that</u> prayer, too!

The same day that Tyndale died, his Bible was being printed—by the king's own printer! Nothing would stop God's words now. And the very next year, the **Coverdale Bible**[1], a *revision* of Tyndale's, was printed by Henry VIII's command!

People would **crowd** around Bibles, just to **hear** God's words. On many nights common farmers kept reading and listening—right until the sun came up. People learned English by reading God's precious Book. **It was water for their thirsty soul** (Psalm 63:1).

Catholic leaders knew **something** had to be done ...

If we want to **recapture** England, we must first **sabotage** Tyndale's Bible!

So we'll create a **counterfeit** Bible, one that **looks** like Tyndale's, but is really **our Vulgate!**

So they did—but in the meantime, God's words were being translated into every language under heaven.

---

[1] Coverdale ended up working on *three* Bibles: Coverdale (1535), Great (1539) and Geneva (1560) . See *Crowned with Glory* by Dr. Thomas Holland (2000), pp. 77-78.

Here is God's Pattern for Preserving His Words:

God wants <u>accurate</u> <u>translations</u> of <u>exact</u> <u>copies</u>.
Then He wants **those translations**
accurately **translated** and **exactly copied**,
and so on down through history…

These translations of God's words in their own native languages are called <u>vernacular</u> Bibles.

Old Latin   German   French   Italian   English

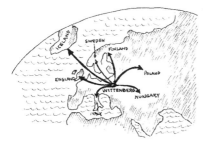

Now **God's words** spread from Germany into **other countries**. And wherever the **true Bible** went, knowledge of the **Gospel** and **Biblical doctrines** went, too.

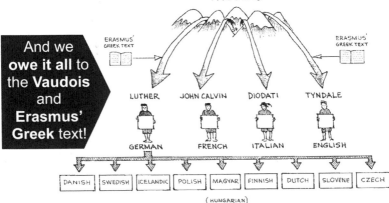

VAUDOIS

ERASMUS' GREEK TEXT

ERASMUS' GREEK TEXT

And we **owe it all** to the **Vaudois** and **Erasmus' Greek** text!

LUTHER   JOHN CALVIN   DIODATI   TYNDALE

GERMAN   FRENCH   ITALIAN   ENGLISH

| DANISH | SWEDISH | ICELANDIC | POLISH | MAGYAR | FINNISH | DUTCH | SLOVENE | CZECH |

(HUNGARIAN)

People rebelled against the Roman Catholic leadership.

You **lied** to us!

God <u>hates</u> idols!

People found out from their **Bible** that the Roman Catholic system had **deceived** them. **Boy,** were they **angry!** In one country after another, they kicked out their archbishops and became Protestants.

The **Bible translators** also wrote **literature for** their country! Education was **no longer** in "**Latin only.**"

THE CATHOLIC LEADERS WERE FURIOUS!
THEIR POWERFUL RELIGION WAS CRUMBLING.

Oh Mary, the **Reformation** is **killing** us!

Your holiness, I have a **man** here who can **solve** our **problem!**

He told the pope about a man who had survived <u>four</u> Inquisitions, **proving** his **love** for the "**Church**" and **Mary,** a man who knew the **secret** of making men obey him, a man who could raise up an army of brainwashed soldiers...

WHO <u>WAS</u> THIS MAN?
LET'S GO BACK A FEW YEARS TO PARIS ...

1528-29 Was an Interesting Year at Montaigu.

It was **one** student's **graduation** year. His name was **John Calvin** (1509-64). But a **dangerous** student was there as well. His name was Don Iñigo de Onaz. We know him today as: **IGNATIUS OF LOYOLA** (1491-1556).

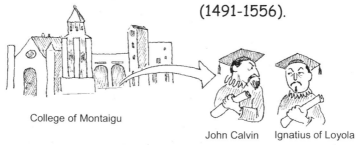

College of Montaigu

John Calvin   Ignatius of Loyola

Ignatius had learned how to *brainwash* volunteers into serving him. He did this with his tiny little book entitled, ***Spiritual Exercises.*** In it a "director" rules the recruit's life, including heavenly *visions—*even his **breathing!** Ignatius met with just **6** fellow students and **two** of them became his top guys: **Salmeron** and **Lainez** (<u>watch</u> them!). Loyola named his band of loyal Catholics:

THE SOCIETY OF JESUS, OR "THE JESUITS."[1]

The Vatican feared Ignatius. He kept building up his forces. They had only two options: **Kill him and all Jesuits**, or **make a deal** with him. Loyola had survived **four Inquisitions.** He wanted to serve the pope.

AND IGNATIUS HAD A PLAN.

WITH JESUITS READY TO OBEY <u>ANY</u> COMMAND, THE COUNTER-REFORMATION HAD BEGUN!

[1] Much of this information comes from *The Secret History of the Jesuits* by Edmond Paris (English translation, 1975). Available from Chick Publications.

1540: LOYOLA REVEALED HIS PLAN TO THE POPE.

> **Holy Father**, let me **build an army of priests** to destroy **all** who oppose our Holy Mother Church! I promise to **obey you**, no matter **what** you tell us to do.

> I want **all nations** to **obey me!** How will you make this happen, Ignatius?

> We will **create schools**. We will be the **advisors** of the **mighty**, and be the **teachers** of their **children. You'll rule the world!**

> **Excellent! I authorize** your Jesuit Order. **Show no mercy!**

Satan thought up a diabolical scheme.

> Who can I **use** to make the **fake English Bible?** Haw haw! **I've got it!**

And the devil decided to create his **English perversion** with the most **unlikely** people in the world.

YOU WON'T <u>BELIEVE</u> WHAT HE DID!

| STEP ONE: | Raise up <u>kids</u> to be Jesuit translators! |

We've got **plans** for you children.

Children were raised in Rheims (and later taken to Douay), France, to be trained in the "art" of translating a counterfeit Bible. They later returned to England as deep agents under Jesuit masters.

Neither their Catholic Rheims New Testament (1582) nor their Douay Old Testament (1610) sold well in England. The true Christians could **tell** it was fake. Step One ended in <u>defeat</u>. **The Devil lost <u>that</u> battle!**

ENGLISH BIBLE

Rheims - Douay

| STEP TWO: | Set up a <u>Council</u> to fight the Reformation. |

This is what **must happen** at the Council of **Trent.**

Agenda for the Council of Trent:

- <u>Not</u> saved by faith <u>only</u>
- Saved by <u>baptism</u> and <u>works</u>
- <u>No</u> Protestants are saved
- Defend <u>Purgatory</u> and <u>Indulgences</u>
- <u>Condemn</u> Protestant Bibles
- <u>No</u> Priesthood of <u>All</u> Believers
- <u>Rome</u> is the mother of all churches
- Defend the "<u>Wafer</u> <u>God</u>"
- <u>Everyone</u> must obey the <u>pope</u>

The pope had to choose carefully who would speak for him at the Council. And who do you think he chose? **Those two Jesuit "fathers," Salmeron and Lainez!**

THE COUNCIL OF TRENT (1545-47, 51-52, 62-63)

Step 2 **worked**. Catholics would soon be walking lock-step with the pope. Something was coming that would WIPE OUT all thought of rebellion among the "faithful." Something was about to experience a revival, that **scared the wits out of young and old.**

SOMETHING CALLED ...

STEP THREE: # THE INQUISITION!

THE HORROR BEGINS

With each council the level of terror increased:

- **1184—Synod of Verona**: Burn heretics at the stake
- **1215—4th Lateran Council**: Burn heretics *and* take their property. The "**Inquisition**" is formed.
- **1220—Inquisition** is handed to the newly-formed "**Dominican**" order.
- **1229—Synod of Toulouse** makes the Inquisition a *systematic* process. Guilty until proven innocent!
- **1252**—Pope "**Innocent**" **IV**: **Torture** is **doctrinally acceptable** to make an accused heretic "confess."
- **1484**—Pope **Innocent VIII** publishes "*Summus Desiderantes*" to support his Inquisitors.
- **1486—Innocent VIII** publishes "*Malleus Maleficorum*" (Witch-Hammer), the systematic guide to detect, torture and execute a suspected "witch." But the deck was stacked against you:
  1. Almost never **see** your accuser
  2. Never **know why** or of **what** you are accused
  3. No lawyer. You have to **prove** your **innocence**
  4. You're presumed **guilty**—*period*
  5. They **promise** *anything*, but **kill** you anyway!

THERE WAS NO PLACE TO HIDE.

GUESS WHO THE CATHOLIC LEADERS INCLUDED AS "WITCHES" AND "HERETICS"?

THE VAUDOIS AND THEIR FRIENDS! WHO ELSE?

1229—The Inquisition **kills 32,000 Albigenses** (friends of the Vaudois) at Toulouse. Their property is stolen.

1487—Innocent VIII promises to **forgive** the sins of anyone who kills Vaudois "heretics." He hands over their **property**, too.

Free property?

Complete **Forgiveness?**

Let's **kill** them!

I've got a **lot** of sins ...

For centuries, Vaudois and other Bible-believers are **hunted down** and systematically **exterminated** by Catholic leaders who are scared of the <u>true</u> Gospel.

After the Council of Trent, Inquisitions spread worldwide. The deaths numbered in the **millions.**

To them, torturing and killing "heretics" was **no worse** than removing a **cancer** from a body.

BUT THERE WAS SOMETHING <u>MORE</u> DANGEROUS TO THEM THAN HERETICS ...

THE WORD OF GOD

Check out this history:

- **1229—Synod of Toulouse** forbids <u>reading</u> or <u>owning</u> a Vaudois Bible. (Canon XIV)
- **1234—Council of Tarragona**: No Bible permitted in one's native language. <u>All</u> of them must be <u>burned</u>.
- **1408—3rd Synod of Oxford**: Heresy to have an "unauthorized" (preserved) English Bible.
- **1559—Council of Trent**: Preserved Bibles are on the "Index of Forbidden Books." (Rule III)

The Inquisition was the devil's excuse to murder **millions** of Christians and destroy their Bibles. But in **2000**, pope John Paul II publicly **apologized** (I think):

Let us ask pardon for the **divisions which have occurred** among Christians, for the **violence some have used** in the service of the truth ...

TRANSLATION:

Ehhh, it was a **little mistake** ...

Just a **few thousand** people and some **books**..

Big deal. They were **only** heretics.

IGNATIUS LED HIS LOYAL ARMY OF ROBOTS AGAINST THE BIBLE-BELIEVING CHRISTIANS

Unknown to the Protestants and Baptists, a secret weapon had been launched against them. The Jesuits worked **undercover** to destroy Protestant Bibles and

Christian schools. Their spies schemed to subvert the most dedicated man of God and turn him into an asset for the Jesuit order.

Jesuits are trained to be patient. They make their plans 50 to 100 years in advance. These covert agents are determined not to fail their masters, even if they lose their lives in his service. And they **never** give up.

ONE NATION STOOD IN THEIR WAY:

We will **never** wipe out Protestants and their Bibles until we destroy **England!**

First we'll make Catholic rulers. **Then** we'll destroy her by Catholic armies. And **finally** we will make sure she switches to **our Jesuit Catholic Vulgate!**

It wasn't going to be easy...

IT WAS TIME FOR A NEW ENGLISH RULER

On **January 28, 1547** King Henry VIII died. The **natural** choice for ruler would have been Catholic **Mary**, his **eldest** child.

But **Henry's will** dictated the order. And **3 days later**, 9-year old Protestant **Edward VI** was crowned king. In the next 6 years Edward authorized **14** editions of English **preserved Bibles** and **35** editions of the **New Testament. What a guy!**

Edward's reign was **short-lived**, however. He caught measles, which weakened him greatly. And in **1553** Edward **died** of **tuberculosis** at 15.

The Jesuits couldn't have been **happier!** For **next** in line was a "faithful" **Catholic** who ruled with an **iron fist**. She **burned** Bible-believers at the stake, including **Bible translators** and many **Reformers**. She was so hateful she was dubbed, **BLOODY MARY!**

Mary wanted to keep the monarchy **Catholic**. To do that, she needed a child. So she married **Philip II, King of Spain**, just to get pregnant and raise a Catholic heir. But it was no use. She had cancer, not a baby.

In 1558 she died, childless. But look who's next!

NOW CAME ELIZABETH'S TURN TO RULE.

Now the 25-year-old Protestant Elizabeth governed England. The pope and the Jesuits were **furious!** They tried everything they could to end her reign—and her **life**. A number of times, **Jesuits** plotted to **kill** her. But **God** wouldn't let them **touch** her.

Then they persuaded Catholic **Mary**, "Queen of Scots," that **she** should be England's queen. But Mary had *other* problems. Her marriage to the evil Henry Stuart was a **disaster**. But **one** blessing came, a son, **James**. In **1567**, Henry Stuart was **murdered**, Mary was **exiled**, and her **1 year old** son **James VI** became Scotland's king .

Mary, "Queen of Scots" and her son, James VI

Mary escaped and fled to England. She was **arrested** and later **executed** for plotting against the queen's life.

> ### No matter how hard he tried,
> ### Satan couldn't dethrone Queen Elizabeth!

So the pope got into the picture. Pius V claimed she was a rebellious <u>Catholic</u> and **excommunicated her** in **1570**. He said no Catholic had to **obey** her anymore. But his whine fell on deaf ears. Sure, English Catholics weren't Protestant—but they weren't **traitors**, either!

Then the Jesuits whispered in King Philip II's ear, "DESTROY ENGLAND WITH YOUR ARMADA!"

King Philip II was proud of his Spanish Armada.

His ships were **feared**, and his navy was **expert** in the art of naval warfare. Philip II plotted to put **Jesuit William Allen**, head of the college of Douay, in charge of England while it was **perverted** back into Catholicism. Then **Edmund**

> **Tell** the Catholics in England to **turn on Elizabeth** as **soon** as **Spain invades**. **We'll** do the **rest**.

> **Yes**, Father.

Campion (another Jesuit) slithered into England with Jesuit missionaries to begin a secret invasion. Yet **God** intervened: Edmund and two other priests were **caught** and **executed**. But a 4th, **Robert Persons**, fled to **Spain** and soon helped plan the Spanish attack of England.

No expense was spared: the pope promised **1 million crowns** to aid Philip. So with 130 ships, 10,000 sailors and 20,000 troops, the war began.

England could only muster **80 ships**, but they were spurred on by their Queen. They were **ready to fight**. But try as they might, they could **hardly** make a **single dent!**

Outnumbered and **out** of **ammunition**, it seemed **nothing** would stop these invaders. But **something did:**

The Spanish Armada was defeated by ... THE WIND!

GOD SENT THE WIND TO DEFEAT THE ARMADA!

Ships were **blown** into the North Sea. Many **sank** in storms or were **dashed** against the **rocks** of the **British Isles**. Troops had **failed** even to <u>set</u> <u>foot</u> in <u>England</u>!

Then Philip got another shock: he never received a **penny** from the pope! Spain was **devastated.** And the Spanish Armada was **never** the same again. It **sank down** while the **British navy rose** into a **world power**.

<u>So the Jesuits **failed** in **every attempt** against England:</u>

- They **failed** to keep a **Catholic** on the throne!
- They **failed** to overthrow even **one Protestant ruler!**
- They **failed** to make the English **Catholics revolt!**
- They **failed** to get **Spain** to **conquer England!**

THE JESUITS WERE <u>BIG</u> <u>LOSERS</u>!

Elizabeth's reign lasted **45 years**, passing away in **1603**. Believe it or not, the **next** in line to the throne of **England** was none other than of Mary of Scotland's **son**! **James VI** of **Scotland** now became **James I** of **England**.

God knew it was time to **perfect** His English Bible. All things were now ready: language, people and king.

GOD WAS SET TO PRODUCE THE <u>KING</u> OF ENGLISH BIBLES!

Chapter Seven:

The King of English Bibles

THE SCOTTISH KING BEGAN TO RULE ENGLAND.

On July 25th, 1603 James began ruling <u>both</u> **England** and **Scotland**. Protestant James had to steer a course between the **Puritans** on **one** side and the **Roman Catholics** on the other, with the "**Church of England**" in dead center. It was a **tough job**!

Puritans had approached James with a **petition**, signed by **1000 pastors**. They wanted a time to address their **grievances** to the king. So James set the date: **January 1604**, at **Hampton Court**.

Bishop Bancroft of London led the **other** bishops, denying **every one** of the Puritans' requests. But when Puritan **John Rainolds** proposed a **new** and completely **accurate Bible**, James was **thrilled**! Bishop Bancroft was **angry,** but not **stupid**. He **listened** to his king.

I want <u>one</u> **uniform translation**, by the **learned** of **Oxford** and **Cambridge, reviewed** by the **chief learned**, and **ratified** by **me**.

This Bible will be **read** in the **whole Church**, and <u>no</u> **other**!

GRRR! The **Puritans** made him do this!

Yes, your majesty.

AND SO A NEW BIBLE WAS BORN.

The translators were set up in three committees:

Westminster	Cambridge	Oxford
1st Company Genesis to 2 Kings	**2nd Company** 1 Chron. to S. of Solomon	**3rd Company** Isaiah to Malachi
5th Company New Testament Epistles	**6th Company** Apocrypha	**4th Company** Gospels, Acts, Revelation

The translators were <u>forced</u> to include the Apocrypha. So they:

- **Stuck it by itself between the Old and New Testaments.**

- **Separated it from the Bible.**

- **Labeled it "Apocrypha" on top of every page!**

The <u>seven objections</u> they listed made it clear: These Alexandrian books are <u>not</u> Scripture!

ROME LOST GROUND AT EVERY TURN.

KING JAMES WAS <u>HATED</u> BY THE VATICAN!

Look, it's a simple request: I want **James** murdered. *Got it?*

I *understand*, your **holiness**.

Robert Catesby, whose priest was a **Jesuit leader**, had previously conspired against **Queen Elizabeth**. Now he got together a band of friends and relatives to **kill King James**, along with most of the **Parliament** (ruling body of England). We know it as the "**Gunpowder Plot**."

Robert Catesby

Thomas Percy

Thomas Wintour

John Wright

Guy (Guido) Fawkes

Catesby's servant **Thomas Bates**

Thomas' brother **Robert Wintour**

John's brother **Christopher Wright**

The plan was simple: Dig a **hole** underneath the Parliament building, **stuff** all the **gunpowder** in, **blow up Parliament**, **kidnap** James' daughter **Elizabeth**, kill his <u>other</u> kids, and make **Elizabeth** into a **Catholic queen**!

<u>WATCH</u> HOW GOD WORKED AGAINST THEM!

The conspirators picked a spot to start digging under Parliament. Suddenly they <u>stopped</u>.

PROBLEM #1—THEY HIT A HUGE <u>WALL</u>!

So they dug *into* it. But one night they were scared by a **loud noise**. Had they been **found?** Nope. It just came from a **cellar parallel** to their own tunnel. So they **quit digging** and **rented** it.

PROBLEM #2—PARLIAMENT <u>DELAYED</u> MEETING!

The Legislature **postponed—twice** (first time till **Easter**, and the second time till **November 5th**). It met almost a **year late!** The **gunpowder** was getting **damp** and unusable. It **had** to be **replaced.** Guy Fawkes had a **key** to the **cellar**, so he had to **sneak** in and **replace** the powder. But that wasn't the **end** of their troubles.

PROBLEM #3—SOMEONE SENT A <u>WARNING</u> OUT!

As if that weren't enough, someone sent a **letter** to Lord Monteagle (a Catholic), warning him **not** to come to **Parliament**. But he **sent** the letter on to the **king!**

NOW KING JAMES WAS ON THE ALERT.

It seemed like they would succeed *anyway*. **Only King James** really knew the danger posed by that letter. His men didn't check under the building till **the <u>day</u> before it met!** And when they saw Guy Fawkes in the cellar by a stack of wood and iron, no one looked **under it!** (Fawkes hid the **gunpowder** there.)

James was **sure** that the powder was there. But he just **barely** got his people to **check again**—at **4 AM!** And there was **Guy Fawkes**, dressed and ready to blow up the building with <u>36 barrels</u> of gunpowder! <u>God</u> had used **King James** to **save Parliament!**

Guy Fawkes **lied** to them, saying he was "John Johnson." He was **quickly arrested** and **questioned**. The **others** heard about it and **fled**. Their evil **scheme fell apart!**

BUT THEY DIDN'T ESCAPE FOR LONG ...

PROBLEM #4—THEIR GUNPOWDER WAS <u>WET</u>!

They re-grouped and got prepared to **shoot** it out. But their powder got **wet**. They tried to dry it off by the fire. But guess what happened? **It**

blew up! It blinded one man and **hurt** four others.

Now they were **filled** with **doubts**. When the sheriff arrived with a **posse**, most of them were **killed. Robert Catesby** crawled to an image of the **Virgin Mary** and died there. Others were rounded up.

Guy Fawkes and **Thomas Wintour** soon **confessed** to their plot. In **1606**, they and their **Jesuit accomplices** were to be hanged.

THE GUNPOWDER PLOT WAS <u>OVER</u>.

Once again the Jesuits **failed**. They didn't get a **Catholic** ruler. So the Bible committees worked **without hindrance** from __anybody__.

GOD CLEARED THE WAY FOR __HIS__ BIBLE.

In 1609 the Jesuits **knew** God's Bible was almost finished. So they quickly **made their move** and published their **complete Rheims-Douay Bible**. But it was __no use__!

Because in **1611** the most __important__ event happened: **GOD'S PRESERVED WORDS were published**, perfectly translated into **English**! Soon King James **held THE BOOK—** which we know as "*The* Bible," "**The Authorized Version**" or simply "**The King James Bible.**"

Within **one generation King James' Bible** was the words of God used by __everybody__—*even the Pilgrims!*

AND SOON THE ENGLISH PROTESTANTS WERE KNOWN AS "THE PEOPLE OF THE BOOK."

BUT THE ASSAULT ON ENGLAND CONTINUED ...

In **1625 King James died**. James' son **Charles I** came to the throne. He was nominally a **Protestant**, but a real **pushover**. His wife was a **Roman Catholic**—a **spy** for the **Vatican**. She actually perverted friends into Catholicism in her own chapel! But that wasn't **all**: Their **lifestyle** was so **expensive** that they almost <u>emptied</u> England's treasury! **Charles I** was **desperate**, so in 1629 he called on Parliament to give him more spending money.

Sire, we **will not** give you the **money**!

NO? Then I shall **dissolve Parliament!**

Charles sought **help** from the **Vatican**. **Jesuit-educated** pope **Urban II** said, "**Of course**, as soon as you become a <u>Catholic!</u>" But even **Charles** knew better than to do **that!**

In the **1640s** his people **revolted**—first the **Scots**, and then **Parliament itself** formed an army against him! **Civil war had begun!** And one man moved from a minor leader to the main commander of the Parliament's army.

HIS NAME WAS <u>OLIVER</u> <u>CROMWELL</u>.

OLIVER CROMWELL'S ONLY KING WAS <u>CHRIST</u>!

He had **no military** training, but he was a great **leader**. Yet his only goal for his godly troops: Get the **king** to **submit to Parliament**.

King Charles I **refused**, but was **defeated in 1646**. Charles promised to **share** power with Parliament, but

he **lied**. With the help of both **Scotland** and **Irish Catholics** he started a **2<u>nd</u> civil war!** But they soon **lost**. Charles was **arrested** and told to **step down** and make his **son** king. Instead he **sent his son away**. So he was tried and **beheaded in 1649**.

The **Parliament** now ran things. But they were **not godly**. They argued, fought and *robbed England blind!*

So Cromwell came **back** to Parliament—**with his army!** He found a bunch of lazy, no-good, totally corrupt **loafers**, not the **Christian** assembly of lawmakers he had planned.

I say it's **time** we had another **pay raise!**

Yes, we deserve it!

Hear, hear!

AND WHAT DO YOU SUPPOSE HE DID?

CROMWELL <u>KICKED</u> <u>OUT</u> THE TROUBLEMAKERS!

The unjust Parliament was disbanded—this time for the **right** reasons. Oliver was offered the **crown**, but he **refused**. He finally accepted the title of "Lord Protector."

Cromwell as Lord Protector:

- **Restored** England to a feared & respected world power
- **Created** the **SPGNE**[1] to send out missionaries
- **Saved the persecuted Vaudois** by threatening armies, raising funds and calling a national fast for God's help
- **Granted freedom** to many Christian groups, which some Congregationalists, Quakers, Baptists & Presbyterians had never known before

AND GOD RICHLY BLESSED ENGLAND.

CHRIST, NOT MAN, IS KING

In **September 1658** Oliver Cromwell **died** and the Vatican **rejoiced**. And in only <u>3 years</u> **Charles II** was <u>back</u>.

He **hated** Cromwell and wanted him to <u>pay</u> for what he did to his father, Charles I. But Oliver was **dead**.

WHAT COULD HE DO TO CROMWELL NOW?

[1] Society for the Propagation of the Gospel in New England

DIG HIS BODY OUT OF THE GRAVE! WHAT ELSE?

In **1661** Cromwell's body was exhumed from the grave, tried, found guilty (just like **John Wycliffe's**) and hung. He then ordered the **head** to be **cut off** and stuck on a **pole** on the top of Westminster Palace.

Charles II

It was on public display for **20 years.** So great was his **hatred** of Oliver and his Puritan friends. But his joy was **short-lived**. He lost **major naval battles** and in **1665** the **Great Plague** hit.

God <u>didn't</u> protect Charles II's London. It was decimated by the "Black Death." Week after week from **1,000** to **6,000** people **died** in those bleak, hot summer months. The very next year the "Great Fire" destroyed **80% of London** over 4 terrifying days. It was **horrible**.

In later years **Catholics** grew **tired** of Charles II and plotted to **kill** him numerous times. As a result, he **arrested** and **executed** some, and **banished** others from Parliament. They were much **happier** in **1685**, when **King James II** plotted to make England **Catholic**. But **this** plan ended in **disaster**. In 3 years he was **banished** and Protestant **William of Orange** took the throne.

AND ONCE AGAIN ENGLAND FOLLOWED GOD.

GOD BROUGHT THE GREATEST MISSIONARY AND REVIVAL MOVEMENTS THROUGH CHRISTIANS WHO <u>BELIEVED</u> & <u>USED</u> THE KING JAMES BIBLE.

Here are a few of these godly men.

John Eliot (1604-90) was the 1<u>st</u> missionary financed by the SPGNE under Oliver Cromwell. He published a **Bible** in the Algonquian Native Americans' language, and planted **14+** churches among them.

John Wesley (1703-91) began the **Methodist** movement. He preached in churches and (illegally) in the **fields** when churches **didn't** welcome him. His preachers went about in "circuits." They preached both **holiness** and salvation by **faith**.

George Whitefield (1714-70) was a friend of the **Wesleys** and the first open-air preacher. He was an **emotional** speaker, yet **clear**. He could bring people to **weeping** with his words, and he could be heard from up to

a **mile** away. **Thousands** got saved—on **2 continents!**

THIS WAS THE "GREAT AWAKENING." IT SPREAD FROM THE BRITISH ISLES TO THE USA.

Jonathan Edwards (1703-58) is known for <u>one sermon</u>.

With a squeaky voice he read his text, "Sinners in the Hands of an Angry God," in a small Connecticut church. **And God moved**. People felt as if they were slipping into **hell** itself as he spoke. **Many got saved**. Society was cleaned up for the next **40 years** by these "soundly saved" Christians.

Francis Asbury (1745-1816) was the first of many Methodist "Circuit Riders." He traveled **270,000** miles and preached **16,000** sermons, even though he was **persecuted** and **rejected** by some. He was always **ready** with **Bible** and **Hymn book**, in **all seasons**.

William Carey (1761-1834) was the Baptist father of modern missions. He lived among the Indians as **one** of them. In 1809 he finished the Bengali Bible. Soon he worked on publishing many more Bibles in other languages.

The 1800s saw **many** revivals like this. And the godly preachers **always** held up the **KJV** as God's **true words**.

Another American preacher helped bring revival ...

Charles Finney (1792-1875) <u>lived</u> for revival.

Once a **lawyer** and a **Mason**, he got **saved** and left them **both** behind. God so **blessed** him he could **not stop preaching** about God. And people got saved left and right. He preached, experienced and wrote on **revivals**. His works were so **powerful** that they even **influenced** a young Christian man to **write a book on revival**, summarizing **Finney's** own **words. That** man was **Jack T. Chick**!

Finney's words have helped <u>generations</u> of people to find revival. And they can work in <u>our</u> day, too.

Adoniram Judson (1804-90) was a missionary to the people of Burma. In **1834** he completed his translation of the Bible into Burmese. Later he spent 21 months in prison during the Anglo-Burmese War. In his life, he took only **one** furlough back home, after **34 years!** Then in the last years of his life, he worked on an English-Burmese dictionary. **What commitment!**

The age that brought the King James Bible was a time of **incredible world missions**, startling stories of **salvation**, of **growth** in the churches and of **preachers** who said, **"Thus saith the Lord" with conviction**, and ...

THE JESUITS SEEMED <u>POWERLESS</u> TO STOP IT!

THE DEVIL <u>FAILED</u> TO DESTROY GOD'S WORDS.

1<u>st</u>, Satan tried
to **destroy** the
Christians' Bibles.

IT <u>DIDN'T</u> <u>WORK</u>!

THE CHRISTIAN CHURCH KEPT GROWING!
They **hid, preserved** and **copied** their Bibles faithfully.

2<u>nd</u>, Satan made a
counterfeit Bible,
in **Greek** then in **Latin**.

IT <u>DIDN'T</u> <u>WORK</u>!

TRUE CHRISTIANS <u>REJECTED</u> THE <u>FAKE</u> BIBLE!

They **only** believed
the **true** Bible
and **spread** it
across the **world**.

3<u>rd</u>, Satan tried to destroy <u>England</u>.

IT <u>DIDN'T</u> <u>WORK</u>!

GOD'S PLAN WAS <u>UNSTOPPABLE</u>!
No rebel, **army** or **ruler** could stop the **KJV**,
God's words in **English**, from **covering** the **earth**.

Yet Satan had <u>one</u> <u>more</u> <u>trick</u> up his sleeve ...

Chapter Eight:
The Jesuits Attack

JESUIT MISSIONARIES WENT EVERYWHERE.

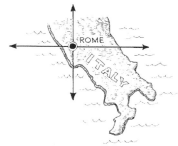

Just **2 years** after the founding of the Jesuit order, their "missionaries" started to **cover the globe**, wreaking **havoc** wherever they went. Soon they **divided** their rule into **six nations** of the world:

ITALY, GERMANY, FRANCE, SPAIN, ENGLAND AND AMERICA.

The Jesuits **didn't mind** various **Catholic** versions of the Bible—*they themselves made the Rheims-Douay!* But they **hated** <u>one</u> <u>Bible</u> with a bloodthirsty passion: **THE KING JAMES BIBLE!** They vowed to **destroy** it.

THIS Bible is our **greatest threat!**

In fact, **one** Jesuit priest spewed **this** hatred at the King James Bible:

"Then **the Bible**, that serpent **which** with head erect and eyes flashing **threatens us** with its venom while it trails along the ground, shall be changed into a rod as soon as we are able to seize it. … **For three centuries past** this cruel asp **has left us no repose**. You well know with what folds **it entwines us** and with what fangs **it gnaws us**."[1]

TRANSLATION:

The Jesuits were scared of the <u>KJV</u>!

---

[1] Hector MacPherson, *The Jesuits in History* (1914), as quoted in *Vatican Assassins* by Eric Jon Phelps (2004), p. 283.

The Jesuits were STILL unable to take England.

Despite the **attacks** and **politics**, England was made able to **stand**. As long as the Christians **believed God's words in English**, the **KJV**, **GOD kept her safe.** Those

Jesuits needed a **plan** to infiltrate England—and fast!

The pope conferred with his Jesuit General.

What is your **plan**, my son?

We **cannot** penetrate England **directly**. So we'll begin in **Paris**, by taking over colleges and seminaries. **Then** we'll take **Germany** ...

IT WAS GOING TO TAKE **200 YEARS** TO ACCOMPLISH!

And so they began. They used both **Jesuits** and **Benedictines**, as they had before with the Inquisition. And soon they were teaching **carefully crafted lies** to the students of **Paris**, starting in the 1670s.[1]

REMEMBER—THE JESUITS ARE NOT JUST *PRIESTS, MISSIONARIES or ASSASSINS,* THEY ARE ALSO <u>TEACHERS</u>!

Tubingen

AND **GERMANY**, THE HEART OF THE REFORMATION, WAS <u>NEXT</u> ...

[1] For more information, see Chapter 9 under "The Master Plan," p. 130.

THE ATTACK ON GERMANY BEGAN ...

The "scholars" will destroy **faith** in God's words, by making them **doubt** that the Bible is true.

Once we do this, we can **wipe out** Protestantism and destroy our *greatest threat*—the King James Bible!

Since the Reformation, Germany's seminaries had been strongly Christian. But Satan was an expert at destroying **faith** with a single question.

Yea, hath God said?

It worked on Eve.
So the devil used the <u>same</u> <u>doubts</u>
to ruin the Christian students.

- Was the Bible *really* inspired by God?
- Did the apostles and prophets *really* write the Bible?
- Is the Bible's history *really* true?
- Is our preserved Bible *really* accurate?
- Did the Catholic church *really* give us the Bible?

  And on and on it went.

Satan only needed to plant the seed of doubt ...

... AND IN CAME THE BIBLE CRITICS!

We're here to <u>help</u> you!

Thus saith the Lord!

The young Bible-believer had **no idea** what he was about to be taught. His professors **looked** Christian—but looks can be deceiving!

The **true** Bible comes from Alexandria, Egypt!

The King James Bible contains **thousands** of errors!

We must find out **which parts** of the Bible are true.

I <u>love</u> my kids!

The young seminary student was taught to **criticize** the Bible's text, history, source, literature and form ...

—but his faith was <u>shattered</u>!

Now I don't know **what** to believe!

NOW IT WAS TIME TO TAKE ENGLAND.

Each tract had a subtle message, to push the Protestant closer to the Roman Catholic system.

The tables began to turn against the Protestants.

---

[1] Much of the information in this section comes from the documented facts found in *The Secret History of the Oxford Movement* by Walter Walsh (1897).

A "Judas Iscariot" was firmly planted in England.°

His name was **John Newman (1801-90)**. John was a deep "mole" who served the Vatican by controlling the Tractarian society. John's brainwashing tactics were so effective that they actually *shifted* the thinking of the English Protestants and drew them closer to Rome.

This is **devastating!**

Newman, you're an **evil genius!**

Remember, our work is **Top Secret!**

Only you guys can know I wrote this.

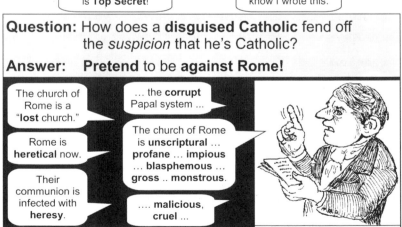

Question: How does a **disguised Catholic** fend off the *suspicion* that he's Catholic?

Answer: **Pretend** to be **against Rome!**

The church of Rome is a "**lost** church."

... the **corrupt** Papal system ...

Rome is **heretical** now.

The church of Rome is **unscriptural** ... **profane** ... **impious** ... **blasphemous** ... **gross** .. **monstrous**.

Their communion is infected with **heresy**.

.... **malicious, cruel** ...

YET NEWMAN WAS ROME'S *BEST FRIEND!*

FINALLY IN 1845 HE REVEALED THE TRUTH.

SURPRISE! I'm **really Roman Catholic! Follow** me to **Rome**, friends and students!

With his disguise off Newman took almost **250** ministers and theologians, and near **625** professors, Parliament members, etc.,[1] to serve the "great whore."

NEWMAN DELIVERED ENGLAND TO ROME!

Just *one year* after he dumped his Christian faith, John was made a **priest**. With his cover blown, he passed leadership of his movement to others. Years later, in **1879** John Henry Newman was given a **privilege** no "regular" priest had **ever** been given. They made him a **Catholic cardinal!**

John Henry **Cardinal** Newman

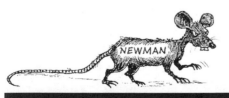

(—Of course, we Bible-believers have **another** name for him.)

AND SATAN'S PLAN WENT INTO HIGH GEAR!

[1] See Earle Cairns, *Christianity through the Centuries* (3rd ed., 1996), pp. 394, 405.

THE DEVIL FINALLY "AXED" THE BIBLE.

Fenton John Anthony Hort
(1825-1901)

Brooke Foss Westcott
(1828-92)

These boys did the dirty work. Both of them were respected professors who moved through high society, rubbing shoulders with occultists and psychics. But these schemers cast their evil eye on God's preserved English Bible. Why? Because they believed in:

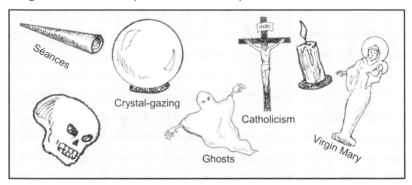

Séances

Crystal-gazing

Catholicism

Ghosts

Virgin Mary

Westcott & Hort also believed in evolution, and held the preserved Bible in utter contempt.[1]

AND IN 1853 THEY BEGAN THEIR EVIL TASK: TO "REVISE" THE KING JAMES BIBLE!

[1] See Appendix B, *The "Faith" of Westcott & Hort.*

"AND LET THE GAMES BEGIN!"

The Church of England gave Westcott & Hort minimal permission to **slightly** change the English Bible —when "necessary." The church gave them an inch ... and <u>they</u> took a mile! Once the work was begun, it was like the foxes entering the hen house ...

CHRISTIANITY WOULD <u>NEVER</u> BE THE SAME.

What in the world did they <u>sneak</u> into the committee?

WHAT DID THEY BRING IN?
THE <u>VATICAN'S</u> COUNTERFEIT BIBLE!

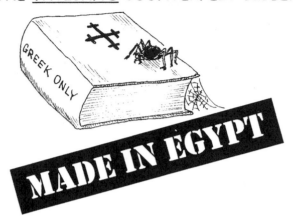

Was this done in the open? They wouldn't **dare**. The committee was shrouded in **secrecy**. Each day pieces of a different Greek text were slipped across the table—which they were **forced** to accept under pressure. Most of them meekly bowed to the demands of Westcott & Hort.

AFTER 28 YEARS OF LABOR, THE CHURCH OF ENGLAND SHOUTED THEIR HALLELUJAHS OVER THIS "NEW AND IMPROVED" GREEK TEXT.

But **was** it new? Well, no ... Here's the guy who **actually** created it.

SURPRISE!

It's our old friend, "Saint" **ORIGEN** (the Roman Catholic church "father"). The Church of England **bought it** ... and the pope was delighted!

The **very next week** in 1881 the Revised Version New Testament appeared. The Bible was almost **totally unopposed** ...

Is there something **wrong** with my King James?

Doubt of God's words spread like **wildfire!**

THE DOOR WAS NOW OPENED WIDE ...

THIS WAS THE BIRTH OF ROMAN CATHOLIC BIBLES CREATED FOR THE PROTESTANT WORLD.

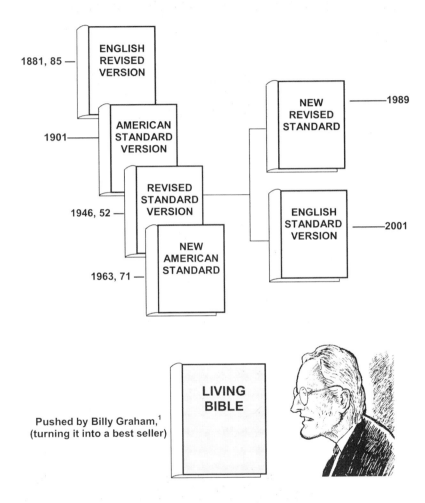

1881, 85 — ENGLISH REVISED VERSION

1901 — AMERICAN STANDARD VERSION

1946, 52 — REVISED STANDARD VERSION

1963, 71 — NEW AMERICAN STANDARD

NEW REVISED STANDARD — 1989

ENGLISH STANDARD VERSION — 2001

Pushed by Billy Graham,[1]
(turning it into a best seller)

LIVING BIBLE

AND THEN CAME THE DADDY OF THEM ALL ...

[1] See Cathy Burns, *Billy Graham and His Friends* (2001), pp. 460-61. Available from Chick Publications

THE KING OF BIBLES— ACCORDING TO EVANGELICALS, CHARISMATICS AND ECUMENICAL LEADERS ALIKE.

We **"scholars"** don't use the *King James Version* in **our** schools. It's *nothing* like Origen's original Greek.

The NIV is the **darling** of almost all of our Christian schools, colleges and seminaries. Most wouldn't **dream** of having a King James Bible in a student's eager hands.

They are taught to hold the KJV in **contempt** as they study books written by Jesuit priests—and are kept totally **ignorant** of Rome's bloody history.

Jesuit

We just LOVE the NIV!

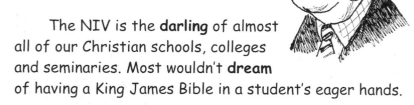

Satan and his Jesuits FINALLY pulled it off.

LOOK AT THE MESS WE'RE IN TODAY...

Chapter Nine:
Look Where We Are Today

"Whoso despiseth the word shall be destroyed"
—Proverbs 13:13

1997: Wealthy media mogul Rupert Murdoch received papal knighthood for promoting the Catholic church and the pope's interests.

NEWS CORPORATION

HarperCollins — Zondervan

Billy Graham's books | **The Satanic Bible**

THIS <u>ROMAN</u> <u>CATHOLIC</u> VERSION[1] IS RUPERT'S BEST SELLER! ➡

NIV ✠

Let's face it: Roman Catholic versions have become <u>big</u> <u>business</u>.

LOOK WHAT IT'S DONE TO BIBLE BELIEVERS...

[1] Bibles based on the perverted Alexandrian/Roman Catholic texts are in reality Roman Catholic Bibles—*with or without the Apocrypha.*

One by one, "Mom & Pop" Christian bookstores are being absorbed by bigger franchises. Many Christian stores are actually *told* what they may or may not sell.

Now big publishers are "educating" many Christian booksellers how to drive customers **away from the King James** and push their own Bible versions.
It's unbelievable!

AND GOD'S PEOPLE ARE THE BIG LOSERS.

If you can't kill the MESSAGE ... kill the MESSENGER!

Would you want to be in _their_ shoes, when they all give account of their dirty deeds before **God Almighty**?

---

[1] For more information, see Appendix A, "For Further Reading."

The warning signs are appearing on all sides...

Some Bible publishers make their commentaries, study guides, lexicons, maps and other Bible helps work **only** with *their* translation. That way, everyone is *re-educated* by the "new" version and the publisher gets richer! No wonder Bible publishing is a huge, multi-million dollar industry!

What does **the Lord** think of this? After all, they are rejecting *the words God preserved in English!*

PASTORS ARE PRESSURED TO DUMP THE KJV.

BIBLE STUDENTS ARE SLOWLY DESTROYED.

"Christian" colleges now turn future missionaries and ministers into *un*-believers!

HOW DID WE GET INTO THIS MESS?!!

IT ALL BEGAN WITH THE "MASTER PLAN" ...

1660s

We have a **Master Plan** to annihilate our <u>greatest</u> enemy ... that @#*%!! **King James Bible**.

It'll take **300 years** to accomplish this task . First, you will infiltrate **secular universities**...

Each step of their plan would take at least **one generation**. They needed to pervert the minds of young **college students**, who would later become **teachers**, and so on ...

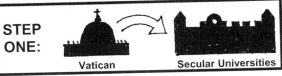

STEP ONE: Vatican   Secular Universities

1670s— 1760s   **Dominicans do the Jesuits' dirty work, spreading lies about the Bible in the Universities of France.**

From the "*Higher Criticism*" of Father **Simon** we <u>all</u> doubt that **Moses wrote** the Pentateuch ...

Father **Mabillon** showed us how to **criticize** the Bible like <u>any</u> <u>other</u> <u>book</u> ...

But Father **Montfaucon** has even **more important** news for us today ...

"*Lower*[1] Criticism" **has proven** that the *Received Text* of the Protestants and Baptists is an **inferior** text ...

... The only **superior** text is one made from **Origen's Bible!**

[1] Also known as "Textual Criticism."

Once "enlightened" schools of France bought into all that "Criticism," the next stop was Germany ...

STEP TWO: Secular Universities → Liberal Seminaries

1800s | Major changes took place. Students brainwashed with Jesuit teachings left the secular universities.

These new professors, guided and coached by Jesuit mentors, would systematically destroy the faith of future pastors. *It was only a matter of time!*

In liberal theological seminaries, **faith** was replaced with **DOUBT**.

When these students graduated, they brought their "Higher Criticism" ... and **doubt** ... with them.

1885 | The English Revised Version (ERV) was published (based on Origen's and other Egyptian manuscripts.

AND A NEW PHASE BEGAN ...

These words came from his **mentor**, someone he **trusted**. And even though **this** teacher wasn't a Jesuit, his **JESUIT TEACHING** passed to the next generation.

STEP THREE:

Liberal Seminaries

Mainline Colleges & Seminaries

1940s The next generation of professors, fresh out of their liberal seminaries, moved into new territory.

I'm going to **Fuller**!

Eastern's the place for me!

Wesleyan College!

I'm **United Methodist**!

The Jesuits' Master Plan moved these men into mainline colleges *and churches*. **All** of them put their faith in their **teachers**—not God's preserved words.

NOW THE IMPOSSIBLE WAS ABOUT TO HAPPEN.

---

[1] By "best" he *really* means Roman Catholic.

STEP FOUR:

Mainline Colleges & Seminaries → Conservative Bible Colleges & Seminaries

1960s The new professors quickly spread their teaching. (None were aware it *really originated* in the Vatican.)

When **these** students graduate, where do you think they will go? Back to their schools and churches!

STEP FIVE:

Conservative Bible Colleges & Seminaries → Fundamentalist schools & Bible churches

1980s

AND NOW LOOK WHAT HAPPENED ...

Once the Christian community lost faith in the King James, they fell for any new version that came along, promising to be **more** "accurate" or "easier" to read. They didn't realize they now read **Catholic** Bibles!

STEP SIX: The Great Falling Away

"For the time will come when they will not endure sound doctrine; but after their own lusts shall they heap to themselves **teachers**" —2 Timothy 4:3

"... Ye shall not **add unto** the word which I command you, neither shall ye **diminish ought** from it...." —Deut. 4:2

THESE MEN ARE GUILTY OF <u>BOTH</u> CRIMES!

WHAT DOES <u>JESUS</u> THINK OF THEM?

These "New Evangelicals," like high priests, are deliberately producing whorish Bibles for their mama.

And here's Mama ... the Great Whore, the mother of harlots, the COUNTERFEIT CHURCH.

IN ONLY 300 YEARS THE DEVIL FINALLY ACCOMPLISHED THE IMPOSSIBLE ...

[1] Matthew 23:33

CHRISTIANS NOW READ <u>HIS</u> <u>BIBLE</u>!

Yes, **he got us.** We've been bamboozled, deceived and betrayed by the "father of lies." And all those new, **counterfeit Bibles** and deceived pastors and teachers are slowly dragging us to Rome.

AND THERE'S ONLY **ONE THING**
THAT CAN BRING US BACK
INTO A REAL, HONEST-TO-GOD
REVIVAL ...

Chapter Ten:
Showdown

WHY NO REVIVAL ?

Let's face the facts. People today are **clamoring** for revival, **claiming** revival, **writing books** about revival, leading **revival rallies**, preaching **revival sermons** and **telling stories** about revival in some remote country ... but one very important FACT remains:

WE HAVEN'T EXPERIENCED A REAL REVIVAL FOR OVER 100 YEARS!

Why? Because we:

- **Trusted our pastors** and not the Bible!
- **Criticized** the Bible, and **refused to believe** it!
- **Turned** from God's words **to man's perverted Bibles!**

SHAME ON US!

TIMES HAVE CHANGED ...

Not too long ago, pastors and teachers spoke God's words with **complete conviction**:

> Thus saith the LORD!

People used to **believe** their KJV and **critique** their **teacher**.

But all that's changed now, thanks to "higher criticism" and "lower criticism" of the Bible. Now people think *backwards*: they **criticize** the **King James** and **believe** their **teacher**!

> Thus saith my TEACHER!

Congregations trust their **preacher**, and college students trust their favorite **professor**. But even the **Apostle Paul** didn't demand people believe *him.* They "searched the scriptures daily, whether these things were so"[1]

> Check for yourselves...

> Look at that! Paul's <u>right</u>!

[1] Acts 17:11

Hmm... how many **revivals** took place from 405-1500 AD using the **Roman Catholic Latin Vulgate?** The same number as there are with the new Bibles: **ZERO!!**

Sounds like a **big difference** to me! Think about this:

If you pour 99% pure water

and add just 1% arsenic,

It will make you 100% dead.

Want to **drink** this water?

"A little leaven leaveneth the whole lump." —Gal. 5:9

YOU HAVE A <u>BIG</u> <u>DECISION</u> TO MAKE ...

DO YOU CHOOSE TO TRUST GOD? OR MAN?

The purpose of this book is to lead you to a choice. The only way for you to make an informed decision is to show you the **truth** regarding **God's words** and **man's**.

HERE IS THE TRUTH:

In reality there are only <u>two</u> <u>Bibles</u>.
- One Bible comes from God through His people.
- The other one comes from the devil through "scholars."

There are also <u>two</u> <u>histories</u>.
- One is the history of God preserving His words.
- The other is the history of man perverting God's words.

And that leaves you with <u>two</u> <u>choices</u>:
1. One is **trusting God**, who <u>preserved</u> His words for you, and trusting His Bible—His words—with all your heart.
2. The other is **doubting God** and **trusting men** who <u>changed</u> God's words to suit their perverted beliefs.

In which of these will you place your complete trust:

---

1. God's blessed and fully preserved words in English, the King James Bible?

OR

2. The ability of "scholars" to decide what they **think** God meant?

EITHER <u>WAY</u>:
YOU WILL HAVE TO FACE JESUS
AND TELL HIM WHY YOU MADE THAT CHOICE!

TRUSTING GOD CAN CHANGE YOUR CHURCH ...

... AND YOUR SCHOOLS

IF YOU ARE WILLING TO PAY THE PRICE ...

YOU WILL BE RIDICULED IF YOU TRUST GOD —AND HIS WORDS.

They will **tempt** you to pick from a pile of **other versions**—every non-KJV Bible they can <u>think</u> of.

Then the world, the flesh and the devil will **attack** you and try to **sink your faith** in God's preserved words.

But your faith is built upon the ROCK of GOD'S WORDS, not the "sandy land" of modern perversions.

JUST REMEMBER:

GOD'S WORDS WILL ALWAYS PREVAIL OVER MAN'S.

GOD BLESS YOU AS YOU MAKE THE <u>RIGHT</u> <u>CHOICE</u>

Appendix A:

For Further Reading

Page 8   Augustine said, "I would not believe the Gospel itself, if the authority of the Catholic Church did not move me to do so." See his *Against the Letter of Mani Called "The Foundation"* (397 AD), 5:6.

For more information about Erasmus, see chapter 6, pp. 66-69 of this book and Erasmus' *Paraphrases Upon the New Testament*, included in Gail Riplinger's *In Awe of Thy Word* CD set. See the Bibliography.

Page 11   For Wycliffe's view on inspiration, see Gail Riplinger's *In Awe of Thy Word* (2003), Chapter 22, pp. 756-760.

Page 18   Regarding Deuteronomy 17: 18-19, see the commentaries of Adam Clark (1831), Jamieson-Fausset-Brown (1871) and John Wesley's *Notes on the Bible* (1765-66).

Page 35   Origen believed God <u>intentionally</u> put errors in the Bible! Read it in his famous work, *De Principiis* (On First Principles), Book 4, Sections 8-19. For a clear translation, see *The Church Fathers on the Bible*, Edited by Frank Sadowski, SSP (New York: Society of St. Paul, 1987), pp. 121-122.

Page 36   Origen's "Septuagint" in Psalm 14:3 **added** 49 Greek words from the New Testament (Romans 3:13-18)! The Catholic *New American Bible, St. Joseph Medium Size Edition* (1977) p. 610, admits this:

> **14,3** Here many Greek and Latin texts ***insert*** the Old Testament quotations which were first combined in Rom 3, 13-18. (*Emphasis mine.*)

So even some Catholics admit that the so-called ***"Septuagint"* wasn't** *actually* written in 285 **BC**. It was clearly written **after 100 AD** by people who had the New Testament *right in front of them.*

Page 40   Peter Allix documents the 120 date in his *Remarks upon the Ecclesiastical History of the Ancient Churches of the Albigenses* (1690), pp. 185-86 (in the Ages Software Library version). The famous 16th century *Geneva Bible* translator **Theodore Beza** agrees.

Frederick Scrivener, in *A Plain Introduction to the Criticism of the New Testament for the Use of Biblical Students,* Vol. II, 4th ed. (1894), p. 43 shows that the Vaudois Bible was dated by historians at no later than 142-157 AD. Amazingly, Scrivener worked *both* on the committee of the Revised Version (1870-81) *and* an edition of the KJV (1866-73).

Page 52   The 1907-14 *Catholic Encyclopedia* (available online or on

CD) contains basic information on Jerome and other major Catholics. The letters between Augustine and Jerome may be found online or in the book *A Select Library of Nicene and Post-Nicene Fathers of the Christian Church,* edited by *Henry Wace and Philip Schaff* (1890-1900).

Page 55   Augustine's *Civita Dei* (City of God) is available in Ages Software's *Master Christian Library*. See the Bibliography.

Page 72   Quotes about Tetzel, some by Martin Luther himself, are available in *The Reformation: A Narrative History* by Hans Hillerbrand (Grand Rapids, MI: Baker Book House 1978 paperback).

Page 81   In *The Reformation Era: 1500-1650* (1965), Harold Grimm documents the positive changes in countries that received the Bible in their native languages. See especially pp. 237-253.

Page 84   A searchable source on Trent is available online: *The Canons and Decrees of the Sacred and OEcumenical Council of Trent* (1848), at Hanover College (http://history.hanover.edu), part of the Hanover College Historical Texts Project.

Page 87   James Plaisted, professor at the University of North Carolina, Chapel Hill, has written a paper posted online, "Estimates of the Number Killed by the Papacy in the Middle Ages." He lists numerous sources over the centuries and weighs the accuracy of the numbers they state.

Page 88   The words in the first cartoon bubble of pope John Paul II are from the *actual words* of his speech made on Sunday, March 12, 2000.

Page 95   The words in King James' mouth are almost a direct quote. See for instance, "King James Onlyism in Scotland" by Dr. Laurence Vance in *The Bible Believers' Bulletin*, December 2004 and "The Origin of King James Onlyism" in the November 2004 issue.

Page 96   The translators' seven objections to the Apocrypha are listed in *Translators Revived* by Alexander McClure (1858), note pp. 185-86 and in *Answers to Your Bible Version Questions* by David Daniels (2003), pp. 139-140.

Pages 97-101 Primary documents on the Gunpowder Plot are available from The Gunpowder Plot Society, at http://www.gunpowder-plot.org.

Page 108   Finney wrote a number of works on revival, such as *Lectures on Revivals of Religion* (1835) and *Letters on Revival* (1845-6, later republished as *Revival Fire*). These works are available online.

Jack T. Chick's book, based on Finney's *Lectures,* is *The Last Call: A Revival Manual* (originally written about 1963).

Page 116   John Newman *knew* he was betraying England to Rome.
See Walter Walsh's *The Secret History of the Oxford Movement* (1897) for
these and many other facts:

- Newman held to Origen's "doctrine of reserve," which means hiding your *true* beliefs from the general public—pp. 1-6.
- He and his friend Pusey schemed for Christians "to find themselves Catholics before they were aware"—pp. 10-11.
- In 1833, *before he started the Tractarians*, he met at Rome with a papal representative. Finding out he could not be officially a *secret Catholic*, he returned to England and decided, "I have a *work* to do in England." This *work* was to give England to Rome.—pp. 262-64.
- One of his closest friends said "his mind was always essentially Jesuitical."—p. 271.

The *Catholic Encyclopedia* (1907-14) under "John Henry Newman" says
his work "broke down the wall of partition between Rome and England."
In other words, Newman was the man that handed England over to Rome.

Page 123   The quickest way to find if a book is written by a Jesuit is to
look for the letters "S.J." after the author's name. However, there are
many Jesuits who don't reveal that they are Jesuits, as well.

There are 4 categories of Jesuits. 3 are "official." The 4th is my own.

Jesuit Type 1: Scholastic—doing his 10-14 years of Jesuit study.
Jesuit Type 2: Priest—finished his study and ordained a Jesuit priest.
Jesuit Type 3: Brother—educated at a Jesuit institution, whether they are Catholic or not. Thousands of Type 3 Jesuits.
Jesuit Type 4: Those educated by Jesuit teachings and methods, but who don't *know* it's Jesuitical. There are millions of Type 4 Jesuits. And *many* teach in Christian schools!

Page 126   This *actually happened* right in front of me. The salesperson
took the KJV from the lady, stuck it under her counter and *told* her to get
an NIV! I was *dumbfounded!*

Page 127   The world was rocked by the *un*founded, *un*documented
slam on King James in the July/August 1985 issue of *Moody Monthly*,
pp. 86-88, "The Real King James." It was followed by a hit piece against
the KJV called "The Bible that Bears His Name," by a Moody Bible
Institute professor. From this point on it became **popular** to slam the KJV
in books and magazines, and to lift up Bibles like the NIV and even the
NKJV—anything that *wasn't* the King James Bible! Stephen Coston
wrote *Unjustly Accused* (1996) to clear James' name.

Pages 130-135 See examples in Grady's *Final Authority* (1993), Ch. 13.

Page 135　So-called Bible "scholars" work on *many* Bibles. But if you put your trust in a "scholar," *which* of his Bible versions will you believe?

Name	NAS 1963, '71	NIV 1973, '78	NKJV 1979, '82	NLT 1996	ISV 1998	ESV 2001	HCSV 2001, '04
Gleason Archer	X	X					
Kenneth L. Barker	X	X					
Frederick Bush	X	X	X				
Harold W. Hoehner	1995U			X	X	X	
F. B. Huey Jr.	X	X					
William L. Lane	X	X	X				
J. Burton Payne	X	X					
Merrill C. Tenney	X	X					
Bruce Waltke	X	X					
William C. Williams	X	X	X				
Herbert M. Wolf	X	X					
Harvey E. Finley	X		X				
Elmer A. Martens	X		X	X			
Moisés Silva	X		X	X		X	
Edward M. Blaiklock		X	X				
Lewis A. Foster		X	X				
Louis Goldberg		X	X				
Walter C. Kaiser		X					X
Meredith G. Kline		X	X				
Douglas J. Moo		X		X	X		
Robert Mounce		X		X		X	R
Barry J. Beitzel			X	X			
Zane C. Hodges			X				X
Eugene H. Merrill			X	X			X
James D. Price			X				X
Allan P. Ross			X	X		X	
Gary V. Smith			X	X			X
Willem A. VanGemeren			X	X		X	
Craig L. Blomberg				X	X	X	R
Gerald Borchert				X	X		
Gary M. Burge				X	X		
Richard Patterson				X			X
Richard Schultz				X			X
John Sailhamer						X	X

NAS=New American Standard, NIV=New International Version, 1995U=NAS 1995 Update,
NKJV=New King James Version, NLT=New Living Translation, ISV=International Standard Version,
ESV=English Standard Version, HCSV=Holman Christian Standard Version, R = Reviewer

Don't put your trust in man's changing opinion.
Trust *only* God's preserved words in English: the King James Bible.

Page 141　The idea for the water and arsenic illustration, as well as the details on the bookstore comic on p. 126, come from Warren Smith and his book, *Deceived on Purpose* (2nd ed., 2004). See the Bibliography for more information on his examination of the "purpose-driven" movement..

The "Faith" of Westcott & Hort

As we have seen, John Newman was the "bridge" between England and the Vatican. But **two men**, Brooke Foss Westcott and Fenton John Anthony Hort, were *the pivotal players in the Jesuits' Master Plan.* They pulled a huge **con job** on us. In 1871 these two walked into their Revision Committee, saying they would *fix* our King James. But in 1881 they came out with a **perverted Alexandrian Bible** instead. The churches fell for it, *hook, line and thinker.* They really believed the KJV had been <u>fixed</u>!

Two decades later in 1901, the American Committee of Revisers published *their* corrections in an "American" form of English.

Soon we had **two** Bibles, both claiming to be the *corrected* word of God: The English Revised Version (ERV, 1881-85) and the American Standard Version (ASV, 1901). Then a *revival* happened! Not a revival of faith—a revival of DOUBT. No one was **sure** he or she knew what God said anymore. **They trusted man's opinion, not God's words**!

In the next decades, more and more Bibles cropped up. A few of them were so-called "revisions" of the ERV or ASV, like these:

- 1946, 1952   Revised Standard Version (RSV)
- 1963, 1971   New American Standard Version (NASV)
- 1989   New Revised Standard Version (NRSV)
- 2001   English Standard Version (ESV)

Some were merely "based on" the ERV or ASV, such as:

- 1965, 1987   Amplified Bible
- 1967, 1971   Living Bible
- 1950-1984   New World Translation (NWT—Jehovah's Witnesses)

Others tried to be "brand new" English translations, including:

- 1926   Moffatt Bible
- 1961, 1970   New English Bible (NEB)
- 1966-1976   Good News Bible (GNB or TEV)
- 1973, 1978   New International Version (NIV)
- 1993, 2002   The Message
- 2001, 2004   Holman Christian Standard Version (HCSV)
- 2002, 2005   Today's New International Version (TNIV)

The Jesuits had a simple goal: to destroy the people of the Book (Protestants and Baptists) by destroying their Book! And Westcott and Hort were the two men that made it happen.

What kind of men were these, who turned the church from God's words to man's opinion? The following quotes will help you to see.

On John Henry Newman, who left Christ for Rome:[1]

Westcott: To-day I have taken up *Tracts for the Times* **and Dr. Newman. Don't tell me that he will do me harm.** At least to-day **he will, has done me good,** and had you been here I should have asked you to read **his solemn words** to me. (Westcott,[2] Vol. I, p. 223—writing to his future wife)

Hort: Many of [Newman's] sayings and doings I cannot but condemn most strongly. But they are not **Newman**; and **him I all but worship.** (Hort,[3] Vol. I, p. 231—writing to Westcott)

My own personal feeling towards Newman has always included **a large share of reverence.** (Hort, Vol. I, p. 423 —writing to his wife after Newman was made a Cardinal)

On Roman Catholicism—as opposed to Biblical Christianity:

Westcott: See Maurice's new lectures, ... He makes a remark which I have often written and said, that **the danger of our Church is from atheism, not Romanism.** (Westcott, Vol. I, p. 43 —in his diary entry for May 8, 1846)

Hort: **Newman certainly raises many thoughts. ... Anglicanism, ... seems a poor and maimed thing beside great Rome.** (Hort, Vol. II, p. 30—after he had read John Newman's autobiography)

We dare not forsake the sacraments or God will forsake us. (Hort, Vol. I, p. 78—written to John Ellerton July 6, 1848)

---

[1] See pp. 116-117.
[2] "Westcott" means *The Life and Letters of Brooke Foss Westcott* by Arthur Westcott (1903).
[3] "Hort" means *The Life and Letters of Fenton John Anthony Hort* by Arthur Hort (1896).

On Mariolatry (the idol–worship of the Catholic Mary):[1]

Westcott:

[Westcott visited a small chapel with an idol of Mary holding the dead Christ.] **Had I been alone, I could have knelt there for hours**. (Westcott, Vol. I, p. 81—written to his fiancée in 1847)

Hort:

I have been persuaded for many years that Mary-worship and Jesus-worship have very much in common in their causes and their results. (Hort, Vol. 2, p. 51)

On Darwin's theory of evolution: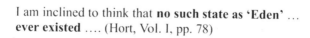

Westcott:

No one now, I suppose, **holds that the first three chapters of Genesis**, for example, **give a literal history**—I could never understand how any one reading them with open eyes could think they did .... (Westcott, Vol. II, p. 69—March 4, 1890)

Hort:

I am inclined to think that **no such state as 'Eden'** ... **ever existed** .... (Hort, Vol. I, pp. 78)

But the book which has most engaged me is Darwin. .... My feeling is strong that **the theory is unanswerable.** (Hort, Vol. I, p. 416—April 3, 1860, the year after Darwin's *Origin of Species* was published)

---

[1] See pp. 55, 57.
[2] See Westcott, Vol. I, pp. 117-119. See also Hort, Vol. I, p. 211.

On their fascination with the occult:

In **1845** Westcott and Hort, with E.W. Benson and 5 others, founded the **"Ghostlie Guild,"** "for the investigation of all supernatural appearances and effects." Others called them the "Cock and Bull Club."

A line from their flyer states:

"But there are many others who believe that the beings of the unseen world may manifest themselves to us in extraordinary ways ....[2]

In **1872** Westcott and Hort, with JB Lightfoot (later a New Testament Reviser with them) founded the **Eranus Club**. Two of its members will soon be involved in the forerunner of the Society for Psychical Research .

Gail Riplinger notes how Westcott, Hort and their friends associated themselves with occultism:[2]

> Pogo sticking through the index of *The Founders of Psychical Research* [by Alan Gauld, 1968] reveals the following 'company' in which our esteemed Bible revisers find themselves.
>
> - Automatic Writing— **EW Benson**
> - Biblical Criticism— **Mme HP Blavatsky** [founder of Theosophy]
> - Clairvoyance, 'Control' Spirit, Crystal-gazing—**Charles Darwin & Sigmund Freud**
> - Ghost Club—**FJA Hort** …
> - Levitation—**JB Lightfoot**
> - Mediumship, Mesmerism, Multiple Personality, Plato, Society for Psychical Research, Spiritualism, Swedenborne Society, Synthetic Society, Telepathy, Trance Medium—**BF Westcott**
>
> (Text reformatted and slightly edited)

---

[1] Westcott, Vol. I, p. 117.
[2] See Gail Riplinger, *New Age Bible Versions* (1993), p. 407.

On the text of the Bible:

> I **hate** the Greek text they used for the King James, "**that vile Textus Receptus!**" [1]

> We'll destroy it with **our own** Greek Text! [2]

> True, but we'd better get our **Catholic Bible** out, **before** they find out what we **really** believe! [3]

> They'll **never know** what **hit** 'em! Haw! Haw! —Then we can **kiss the Protestants goodbye!**

These are the men who made *shipwreck* of the faith of millions.

Now you know the truth. Are *you* going down with the ship?

[1] See Hort, Vol. I, p. 211.
[2] See Westcott, Vol. I, pp. 228-229.   [3] See Hort, Vol. I, p. 445.

PRINT MEDIA

Burns, Cathy. *Billy Graham and His Friends.* Mt Carmel, PA: Sharing, 2001. A thoroughly documented book about Billy Graham's beliefs and how they have been compromised over the years.

Cairns, Earle E. *Christianity through the Centuries,* 3rd edition. Grand Rapids, MI: Zondervan, 1996. Basic church history text for Bible colleges. Now uses the perverted NIV and buys into Biblical criticism—to a point.

Chick, Jack T. *The Force.* Ontario, CA: Chick Publications, 1983. Crusader Comic # 15, revealing the occult side of the Great Whore of Revelation.

Chick, Jack T. *Sabotage?* Ontario, CA: Chick Publications, 1979. Crusader Comic #11, summarizing how Egypt and Rome created a counterfeit Bible.

Chick, Jack T. *The Last Call: A Revival Manual.* Ontario, CA: Chick Publications, 2003. Originally written in 1963. Summarizes Finney's *Revival Lectures* in an easy-to read format, with descriptive comics to aid the reader.

Daniels, David W. *Answers to Your Bible Version Questions.* Answers 60 of the main questions asked about the Bible version issue.

Dowley, Tim, editor. *Introduction to the History of Christianity.* Minneapolis: Fortress Press, 1990. The most popular church history textbook I know of. A thorough overview of Christian history as it is being taught today. Wrongly assumes Catholics are Christians and Baptists are a recent development.

Foxe, John. *Acts and Monuments.* The original 1583, multi-volume text written by John Foxe. Available in Gail Riplinger's *In Awe of Thy Word* CD set. Note: every one-volume "Foxe's Book of Martyrs" was NOT written by Foxe. It's a summary. Some are more accurate than others. Some wrongly add Catholic "martyrs."

Grady, William P. *Final Authority: A Christian's Guide to the King James Bible.* Schererville, Indiana: Grady Publications, 1993. Excellent Bible history book.

Grimm, Harold. *The Reformation Era 1500-1650, with a Revised and Expanded Bibliography.* New York: Macmillan Co, 1954, 65. Has information about the Reformation I've not found compiled anywhere else.

Holland, Thomas. *Crowned with Glory: the Bible from Ancient Text to Authorized Version.* San Jose: Writer's Club Press, 2000. His readable book is available in the Swordsearcher Software. See below.

Hort, Arthur. *The Life and Letters of Fenton John Anthony Hort.* 2 Vols. London: Macmillan Co., 1896. You learn a lot from reading someone's letters!

Hunt, Dave. *A Woman Rides the Beast.* Eugene, OR: Harvest House, 1994. Shows how the Roman religion fulfills Revelation 17-18's Whore of Babylon.

Ignatius of Loyola. *Spiritual Exercises.* New York: Doubleday/Image, (1964). The text used in a careful program to turn volunteers into Catholic robots.

Josephus. *Against Apion.* Part of the Ages Software *Master Christian Library.* See below.

McGrath, Alister. *In the Beginning.* New York, Anchor Books, 2001. A non-King James believer writing a history of the King James. Beware of his biases.

Moynahan, Brian. *God's Bestseller.* NY: St. Martin's Press, 2002. Tells the truth about Thomas More and the move against Tyndale's preserved Bible.

Paris, Edmund. *The Secret History of the Jesuits.* English translation. Ontario, CA: Chick Publications, 1975. A quick summary of Jesuit history and belief.

Phelps, Eric Jon. *Vatican Assassins.* Newmanstown, PA: Eric Jon Phelps, 2001, Electronic Edition 2004. Has information you will find *nowhere* else.

Riplinger, Gail. *In Awe of Thy Word.* Ararat, VA: AV Publications, 2003. A humongous compilation of history and linguistic proofs for the KJV!

Ruckman, Dr. Peter S. *The History of the New Testament Church.* 2 Vols. Pensacola, FL: Bible Baptist Bookstore, 1982. History as only Dr. Ruckman can tell it.

Sadowski, Frank, editor. *The Church Fathers on the Bible.* New York: Society of St. Paul, 1987. What some Catholic "fathers" thought about the Bible.

Smith, Warren. *Deceived on Purpose,* 2nd ed. Magalia, CA: Mountain Stream Press, 2004. The "dark side" of the Purpose-Driven movement. For more information, call (866) 876-3910.

Tixeront, Rev. J, Translated by S.A. Raemers (English Edition). *Handbook of Patrology.* St. Louis, MO: B. Herder Book Co., English Edition, 1920.

Walsh, Walter. *The Secret History of the Oxford Movement.* London: Swan Sonnenschein & Co., 1897. Excellent documentation, from *Catholic* sources!

Wells, H.G. *The Outline of History.* Garden City, NJ: Garden City Books, 1961.

Westcott, Arthur. *The Life and Letters of Brooke Foss Westcott.* 2 Vols. London: Macmillan & Co., 1903. These letters are *very* revealing.

ELECTRONIC MEDIA
Ages Software. Master Christian Library, Reformation Library and others. Available at www.ages.com

Catholic Encyclopedia, 1907-14. Available at www.newadvent.com.

In Awe of Thy Word **CD ROM set.** Available at www.avpublications.com.

Sola Scriptura Publishing. Amazing source for many Bible-related out-of-print books. See www.solascripturapublishing.com for current titles.

Swordsearcher Software. Bible program with many books, dictionaries and commentaries. See www.swordsearcher.com for more information.

Subject Index   157

Gunpowder Plot 97-100, 146
Gutenberg, Johannes 64-65

H
Habakkuk (book of) 26-27
Haggai (book of) 26, 27
Hampton Court 95
Hebrews (book of) 13, 28, 64
Henry VIII 68, 79, 90
Higher Criticism 130-131, 140
Holland, Thomas 79
Hort, Fenton John Anthony 118-122,
  149-153
Hosea (book of) 26
Hunt, Dave 51

I
Idol/Idolatry 6, 20, 55, 81, 151
Inquisition 72-73, 81-82, 86-88, 112
Inspiration/Inspired 11, 113, 145
Irenaeus 56
Isaiah (book of) 25, 27, 96
Israel 15, 18, 19, 20, 25, 26, 27, 31, 39,
  55
Israelite(s) 12, 14, 21,

J
James I (King of England) 91, 93, 95-
  99, 101-106, 146, 127, 147
James II (King of England) 105
James (apostle) 29, 56
James (book of) 28, 29
Jeremiah (book of) 25
Jerome 41, 51-53, 55-57, 146
Jerusalem 20, 21, 25-27, 29, 31, 39
Jesuit(s) 82-85, 89-93, 97, 100-102,
  108, 110-114, 123, 130-132, 147, 149
Jesus Christ 22, 24-25, 28-29, 35-36,
  64, 115, 129, 135, 137, 142, 151
Jesus (fake) 55, 82
Job (book of) 22, 23, 24
Joel (book of) 26
John (books of) 28, 29,
John (disciple) 29
John Paul (pope) 77, 88, 146
John the Baptist 27

Johnson, John 99
Jonah (book of) 26, 27
Josephus 17
Joshua 15, 19, 24
Jude/Judas (Jesus' 1/2 brother) 28-29,
  56
Jude (book of) 28, 29
Judges (book of) 19
Judson, Adoniram 108

K
King James (Bible) 101, 106-108, 111,
  113-114, 118, 121,123, 126, 128, 130,
  132-134, 140, 142, 146-149, 153
KJV 64, 107, 109, 111-112, 123, 128-
  129, 132, 140, 144-145, 147, 149

L
Lamentations (book of) 25
Latin, Old 39-41, 51-54, 59, 61, 69, 73,
  80
Law of Moses 12, 14-15, 18, 21, 24
Levite(s) 14-18
Leviticus (book of) 14
Living Bible 122, 149
Lower Criticism 130, 140, 145, 152
Loyola, Ignatius of 82-83, 89
Luke (book of) 22, 28,
Luke (disciple) 28, 56
Luther, Martin 71-73, 75, 77, 146

M
Mabillon, Jean 130
MacPherson, Hector 111
Mainz, Germany 64-66
Malachi (book of) 26, 27, 96
Mark (book of) 28, 29, 59
Mark (disciple) 28, 29,. 56
Mary (bloody Queen) 90
Mary (fake Virgin) 55, 57, 81, 100,
  118, 151
Mary (mother of Jesus) 28, 29
Mary, Queen of Scots 91, 93
Master Copy 16-18
Master Plan 112, 130-137, 149
Matthew (book of) 9, 28, 29, 136

ALSO BY DAVID W. DANIELS

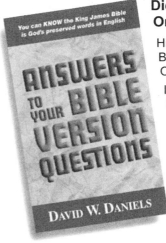

Did God preserve His words?
Or does my Bible contain errors?

History shows there are two streams of Bible texts, and they are not the same. Obviously, both cannot be correct.

In this book, respected linguist David Daniels proves we can know that the King James Bible is God's preserved words in English, by answering many difficult questions the so-called experts throw at the King James.

If you want to defend the KJV or learn which Bible you can trust, the answers are here.

Questions include:
- Wasn't the King James Bible translated from only a few late manuscripts?
- Has the King James Bible been changed between 1611 and the present?
- Is it good enough that the missing words in my NIV are in the footnotes?
- Don't Bibles with different words still say the same thing?
- What proof do you have that the Sinaiticus was found in a wastebasket?
- Has God only preserved a Bible for English-speaking people?
- What is wrong with the New King James Version?

AND:

The King James Bible Companion

This small booklet has the definitions of over 500 less familiar KJV words. Tuck it inside your King James Bible for easy reference. Give them out at Bible Studies, Youth Groups, Sunday School classes, Christian Schools, etc.